100

THINGS TO DO IN
WASHINGTON, DC
BEFORE YOU
DIE

2ⁿᵈ Edition

100

THINGS TO DO IN
WASHINGTON, DC
BEFORE YOU
DIE

KATIE BIANCO

REEDY PRESS

Library of Congress Control Number: 2018945636

ISBN: 9781681061689

Design by Jill Halpin

Author cover photo: Greg Powers

Printed in the United States of America
18 19 20 21 22   5 4 3 2 1

Please note that websites, phone numbers, addresses, and company names are subject to change or cancellation. We did our best to relay the most accurate information available, but due to circumstances beyond our control, please do not hold us liable for misinformation. When exploring new destinations, please do your homework before you go.

DEDICATION

For Anthony.
Exploring this city is even better with you by my side.

... and for Ellie and Teddy.
So many Washington, DC adventures await you.

Courtesy of Tiny Jewel Box

CONTENTS

● ●

• •

Sports and Recreation

Culture and History

• •

• •

● ●

PREFACE

For many years, DC was known as a company town. The nation's capital was in the business of the federal government, and a vacation here was seen as more of a patriotic duty. I'll hear from people who say they came to see the city's imposing marble monuments and memorials on a class trip in seventh grade and haven't returned since.

100 Things to Do in Washington, DC Before You Die makes the case that DC's reputation as a stuffy town meant only for buttoned-up politicos no longer applies. Today, the District of Columbia ("the District," as locals often refer to it) is a celebrated city with a diverse mix of critically acclaimed restaurants, fashion-forward retail, cutting-edge arts and culture, and family-friendly fun. DC is definitely a destination worth visiting, and this book outlines all the must-dos if you're looking to get to know the nation's capital beyond the borders of the National Mall. Sure, if you've never been here before (or only been as a fanny pack-wearing seventh grader), a day or two spent exploring our iconic monuments, memorials, and museums is a must. There's still nothing quite like driving down Constitution Avenue and seeing the Washington Monument for the first time or stepping into the Smithsonian National Air and Space Museum's cavernous main hall. But the suggestions in this book also encourage you to discover the DC that locals know and love. Whether dining at a hot spot along the bustling Fourteenth Street corridor, listening to live jazz on a summer night at the National Gallery of Art's Sculpture Garden, or living out your fashion fantasy at CityCenterDC, you're sure to find something in this book to add to your own bucket list.

I've lived in the DC region for nearly forty years, and I've been writing about the city professionally for more than fifteen. The suggestions in this book are based on many years of exploring my hometown, interviewing locals and experts, and even casually polling my friends. There's so much to see and do in DC, and I'm excited to share this great town with you. I'd also love to hear what your favorites are. Let's chat on Twitter and Instagram @KatieBiancoDC.

Welcome to DC!

ACKNOWLEDGMENTS

I wouldn't have written this book if it weren't for my former colleague at Destination DC, Robin McClain, who connected me with the team at Reedy Press. It's been a pleasure to work for you and with you as cheerleaders for this city over the years. Thank you to Kate Gibbs as well, another former Destination DC colleague and all-around DC expert, for your always great ideas.

I've been writing about DC for more than fifteen years and have had the pleasure of working with a number of wonderful editors along the way. Thanks to all who've helped me grow as a writer and see the city in new ways.

I'd also like to thank the people of DC—all the artists, restaurateurs, entrepreneurs, designers, politicos, and more—who make this city tick. It's been a pleasure telling your stories.

To all my hometown friends who've explored DC with me—first as kids on field trips, then as single gals taking on the city in our twenties, and now all my fellow parents discovering the family-friendly side of DC.

For my husband. I wrote the first half of this book while in my third trimester and the second half while on maternity leave with a fussy newborn. If it weren't for your hands-on parenting while I furiously typed away on my laptop, I would have never

• •

finished. Sightseeing with you for book research was fun, too. There's no one I'd rather explore this city with.

Finally, I want to thank my mom. She's been gone ten years, but she instilled in me a deep and abiding love for Washington, DC. She moved here after college in the 1960s from a small town in Indiana to be a reporter and she never looked back. She was known to shed a tear or two of joy when she drove past the monuments along the GW Parkway. That's how beautiful she found this city. It's because of her that I'm both a writer and completely in love with DC.

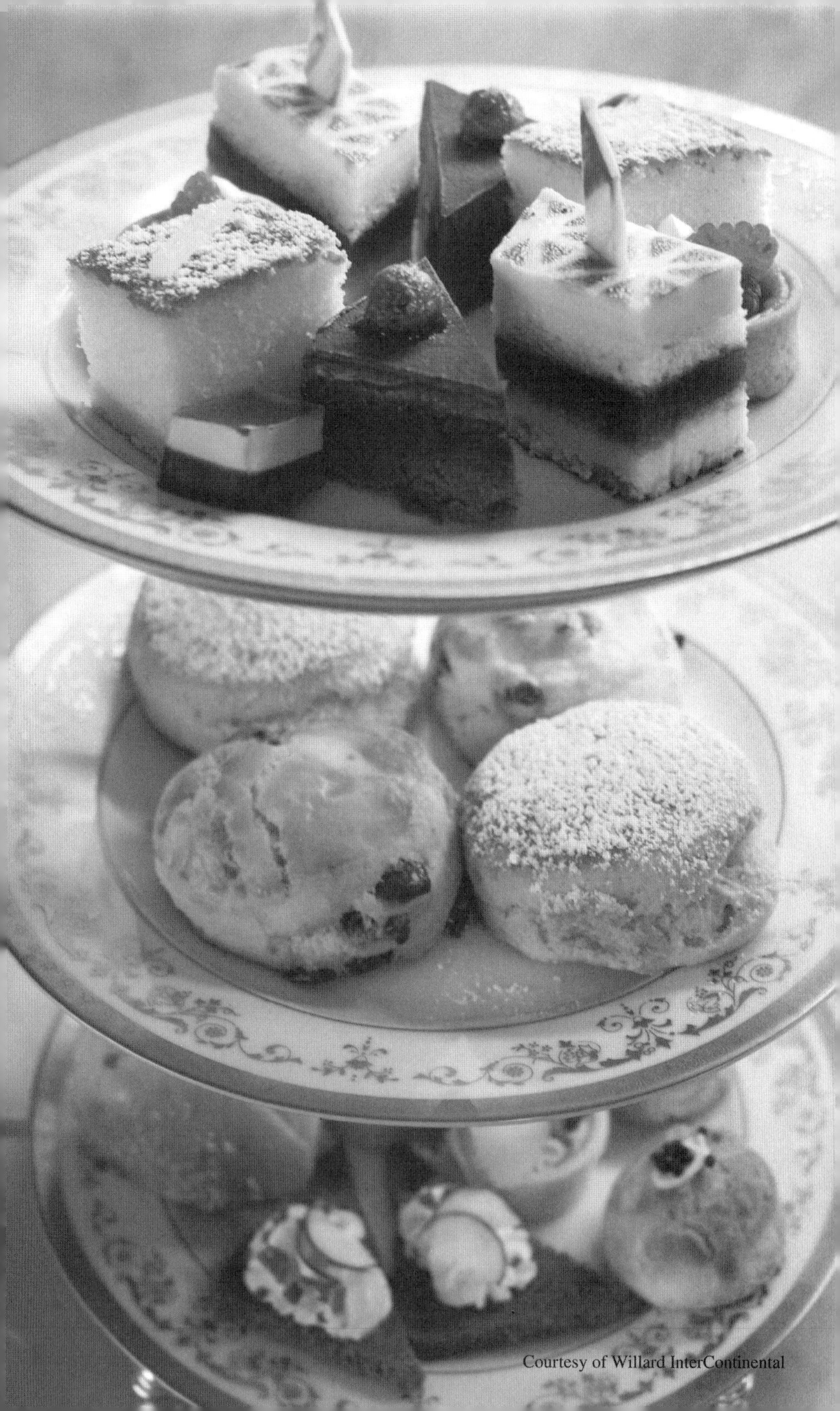

Courtesy of Willard InterContinental

FOOD AND DRINK

STEP BACK IN TIME
AT DC'S OLDEST SALOON

Not many places are as beloved by DC's political class and out-of-towners alike, but Old Ebbitt Grill manages to attract both. The popular restaurant actually stakes its claim as the oldest saloon in Washington, DC, at more than 160 years old (with several location changes throughout the years) and has a rich history of hosting presidents as far back as Andrew Johnson. Today, Old Ebbitt is located near the White House and still sees plenty of political movers and shakers in its midst. Look for them talking shop in the Victorian-era dining room awash in artwork that depicts classic DC or grabbing drinks at the taxidermy-bedecked mahogany bar. Legend has it that the animal heads presiding over the patrons were bagged by Teddy Roosevelt himself.

Old Ebbitt Grill
675 Fifteenth St. NW, 202-347-4800
ebbitt.com
Metro: Metro Center (Red, Orange, Blue Lines)

TIP
Old Ebbitt is also famous for its fresh oyster selection. A dedicated Oyster Bar is the place to sit and try its signature platters. Want to go all in? Each year on the Friday and Saturday before Thanksgiving the restaurant hosts its raucous Oyster Riot, a veritable oyster feast.

SAMPLE ONE OF DC'S SIGNATURE FOODS
AT BEN'S CHILI BOWL

It's fair to say that you haven't really been to Washington, DC, until you eat at Ben's Chili Bowl. Open since 1958, the DC institution serves up its famous Chili Half-Smoke (that's a pork and beef smoked sausage with mustard, onions, and Ben's spicy homemade chili sauce on a steamed bun) from its enduring perch on U Street. Ben's has made a name for itself beyond the borders of Washington, DC, and has welcomed an array of famous faces, from Dr. Martin Luther King Jr. and Duke Ellington in the early days to Denzel Washington, Bono, and even Barack Obama in recent years. Go to see the framed photos of famous patrons—but mostly visit because the chili is so good.

Ben's Chili Bowl
1213 U St. NW, 202-667-0058
benschilibowl.com
Metro: U Street (Yellow, Green Lines)

TIP
Be sure to check out the mural in the alleyway next to Ben's. Painted by DC artist Aniekan Udofia, it features various celebs, including Muhammad Ali, Prince, Michelle Obama, Dave Chappelle, and Roberta Flack.

DINE AT DC'S
MICHELIN-STARRED RESTAURANTS

For years, the nation's capital was strictly a steakhouse kind of town. The political class did their wheeling and dealing in restaurants that involved thick cuts of meat and dimly lit dining rooms. Eventually, though, a few talented chefs took a chance on the city, and today DC and dining go hand in hand. It's been getting accolades for a number of years, including being dubbed Restaurant City of the Year by *Bon Appetit* magazine in 2016, but it was when Michelin came calling that DC's status as a powerhouse culinary city was truly cemented. One of only four U.S. cities to receive stars from the world-famous reviewer, DC is a must for any true foodie. The 2018 rankings include eleven restaurants earning one star, while three restaurants picked up two stars. Make reservations for one or eat your way through all fourteen—but definitely don't miss your chance to dine at one of DC's finest.

guide.michelin.com/us/washington-dc

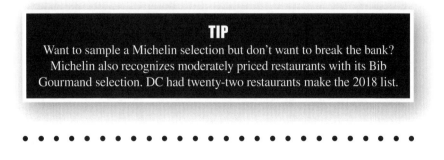

TIP
Want to sample a Michelin selection but don't want to break the bank? Michelin also recognizes moderately priced restaurants with its Bib Gourmand selection. DC had twenty-two restaurants make the 2018 list.

RAVE REVIEWS

Make your reservation at one of these Michelin-approved restaurants:

TWO STARS

minibar (See page 20 for more details.)
minibarbyjoseandres.com

Pineapple and Pearls
pineappleandpearls.com

The Inn at Little Washington
theinnatlittlewashington.com

ONE STAR

Blue Duck Tavern
blueducktavern.com

Fiola
fioladc.com

Kinship
kinshipdc.com

Komi
komirestaurant.com

Masseria
masseria-dc.com

Metiér
metierdc.com

Plume
plumedc.com

Rose's Luxury
rosesluxury.com

Sushi Taro
sushitaro.com

Tail Up Goat
tailupgoat.com

The Dabney
thedabney.com

GET A TASTE OF THE SWEET LIFE
AT GEORGETOWN CUPCAKE

Sisters Katherine Kallinis Berman and Sophie Kallinis LaMontagne opened their cupcake shop in a charming shoebox of a space in Georgetown in 2008 to near-immediate success. Fast-forward a decade and they've not only moved to a prime spot on Georgetown's famous M Street (plus added a location in nearby Bethesda, Maryland), but they also have a TLC reality show under their belts, two cookbooks, and four more storefronts across the country. Even as the cupcake craze wanes, the Georgetown hot spot still sees an almost constant line spilling out the door (even on rainy days!) made up of local college students, out-of-towners, and Washingtonians looking to satisfy their sweet tooth. Pop in for one of their famously delicious cupcakes featuring such fun flavors as Vanilla Birthday or Red Velvet and their signature fondant flower adornments.

Georgetown Cupcake
3301 M St. NW, 202-333-8448
georgetowncupcake.com
Metro: Foggy Bottom-GWU (Orange, Silver, Blue Lines)

SWEET SHOPS

Georgetown Cupcake isn't the only local baker in town. Pick up some sweet treats at any of these homegrown bakeries:

Baked & Wired
1052 Thomas Jefferson St. NW, 703-663-8727
bakedandwired.com

Buttercream Bakeshop
1250 Ninth St. NW
buttercreamdc.com

Buzz Bakeshop
Locations in Arlington and Alexandria, Virginia
buzzbakeshop.com

TIP

Want to skip the line at Georgetown Cupcake? Order online by 5:00 p.m. the day before and proceed directly to the counter upon arrival.

EAT PANCAKES
WITH POLITICAL HEAVYWEIGHTS

DC is a town that doesn't waste the day. You'll find politicians, lobbyists, dignitaries, and more meeting to discuss policy issues over breakfast as the sun is coming up in restaurants all over town. One of the most well-known networking breakfast spots is Seasons restaurant at the Four Seasons Hotel in Georgetown. The dining room is tucked inside the luxury hotel and offers a discreet place for sensitive discussions and hearty handshakes. Get there early—the dining room opens at 6:30 a.m. on weekdays—if you want to play "spot the politician" before they head into their offices. Famous faces seen dining here over the years include Hillary Clinton, Condoleezza Rice, Madeleine Albright, and John McCain. Hollywood celebs staying at the hotel, such as Tom Hanks, Jay-Z and Beyonce, and George Clooney, have even been known to break bread at the morning hot spot. Order the popular lemon ricotta pancakes and see who you can peep.

Seasons
Four Seasons Hotel Washington, DC
2800 Pennsylvania Ave. NW, 202-342-0444
fourseasons.com/washington/dining/restaurants/seasons/
Metro: Foggy Bottom-GWU (Orange, Silver, Blue Lines)

FEAST ON NATIVE FOODS
AT THE NATIONAL MUSEUM OF THE AMERICAN INDIAN

The Smithsonian's National Museum of the American Indian explores the rich history of indigenous people throughout the Western Hemisphere by looking at their lifestyle, art, history—and even food. The Mitsitam Native Foods Cafe (*mitsitam* means "let's eat" in the native languages of the Piscataway and Delaware people) serves foods reflective of cultures across the Americas—from the Northwest Coast to the Great Plains to South America. It's worth planning your lunch around this authentic cafeteria-style restaurant, which sources many of its ingredients from tribal companies or co-ops. Of course, a stop at the cafe is just part of the experience. The Smithsonian museum features four levels of exhibitions and activities. Start in the soaring Potomac Atrium, featuring a skylight that on sunny days reflects rainbow light refractions on the first floor.

Mitsitam Native Foods Cafe
National Museum of the American Indian
Fourth St. & Independence Ave. SW, 202-633-1000
mitsitamcafe.com
Metro: L'Enfant Plaza (Orange, Silver, Blue, Yellow, Green Lines)

GET A BIRD'S-EYE VIEW OF THE WHITE HOUSE
AT POV

Unless you score an invite to a state dinner at the White House, having a cocktail at POV, the W Hotel's posh rooftop lounge, is the next best thing. The lounge is known as a see-and-be-seen hot spot in DC thanks mostly to its proximity to 1600 Pennsylvania Avenue. Reserve a booth or a spot at the bar that overlooks the White House and you'll be so close you'll be tempted to try and peek in the windows. If you're lucky, you may even catch Marine One landing on the lawn, an event that always creates a stir on POV's terrace. The decor pays tribute to the Washington bureaucracy, but in a super-sexy way. Look for the forty-foot "red tape" wall as well as modern murals that give a nod to the Declaration of Independence and the gift of the cherry blossoms. Most nights you'll find a DJ or live musicians playing a set in the lounge. Reservations are strongly encouraged if you want to mix and mingle with DC's cocktail crowd—and definitely come dressed to impress.

POV
W Washington DC
515 Fifteenth St. NW, 202-661-2400
povrooftop.com
Metro: Metro Center (Red, Orange, Blue Lines)

SAMPLE FRESH AND LOCAL FOODS
AT UNION MARKET

You'll want to come hungry to Union Market. With more than thirty food stalls to choose from, sampling delicacies is the name of the game. Located in an industrial area of Northeast Washington that's seen a rapid gentrification in recent years, Union Market anchors the up-and-coming neighborhood. The vast space, which was a thriving fresh food market in the sixties and seventies, got a facelift and reopened its doors about six years ago. Today, you'll find a mix of hipsters sipping cocktails, moms with strollers meeting up for coffee, college students, and more hanging out in this always bustling community. Union Market includes local faves, such as Takorean, Buffalo & Bergen, Trickling Springs Creamery, and Red Apron Butcher, along with a handful of retail options and sit-down restaurants. Bring your laptop and settle in for an afternoon of eating and people watching.

Union Market
1309 Fifth St. NE
unionmarketdc.com
Metro: NoMa-Gallaudet U (Red Line)

HAVE A BEER
WITH LIZ TAYLOR IN SHAW

On evenings and weekends during the warmer-weather months, you'll find Washingtonians spilling out of a postage stamp–sized outdoor bar in DC's Shaw neighborhood. Started by two college buddies, the food and drink list is modeled after the traditional Bavarian beer gardens in Germany. Belly up to one of the picnic tables and select from a menu of Belgian and American craft beers, plus local meads and ciders, cocktails, and wines. A selection of brats adds to the authenticity, and it's all served under the shadow of a four-story mural of Elizabeth Taylor. When the bar, called Dacha, moved in, the owners wanted to create an icon for the up-and-coming neighborhood. They selected Liz Taylor because of her longtime dedication to DC-based Whitman Walker Clinic, a nonprofit organization active in the fight against HIV/AIDS. It's a worthy reason indeed, but in the summer, you'll likely only notice Taylor's sexy sizzle looking down on you.

Dacha Beer Garden
1600 Seventh St. NW, 202-350-9888
dachadc.com
Metro: Shaw-Howard U (Yellow, Green Lines)

PAINT THE TOWN

Liz Taylor is just one of many murals making their mark all over DC. If you're in search of some Instagram-worthy artwork, check out these four other outdoor art locations:

Marilyn Monroe
by John Bailey
above Salon Roi in Adams Morgan
2602 Connecticut Ave. NW

Marvin Gaye
by Aneikan Udofia
near the African American Civil War Memorial in Shaw
711 S St. NW

Heart Wall
by Mr. Brainwash
at Union Market
1309 Fifth St. NE

Penguin at the Wharf
by No King's Collective
at the Wharf
Blair Alley between Wharf St. and Maine Ave. SW

TIP

You don't have to wait for warmer weather to try Dacha Café. Located just next store, the bagel shop focuses on born-in-DC brands. Get a taste of the local culinary entrepreneurs here, such as Bullfrog Bagels and Zeke's Coffee.

FEEL LIKE YOU'RE ON THE MEDITERRANEAN
AT THE GEORGETOWN WATERFRONT

Husband-and-wife restaurateur team Chef Fabio and Maria Trabocchi have built a culinary empire in DC with five critically acclaimed restaurants dotting the DC map, including Fiola, Del Mar, and Casa Luca. Inspired by the couple's Mediterranean roots, their Georgetown waterfront restaurant, Fiola Mare, is well worth the splurge. The Bidens, Michelle Obama, Pierce Brosnan, and Steven Tyler have all been spotted dining in this see-and-be-seen restaurant, but it's the delectable menu and seaside feel that make it a must. Come hungry and start with the pricey but plentiful seafood platter, the San Benedetto. Simple fish entrées and pastas also evoke a traditional Mediterranean meal, while the restaurant's version of the Negroni is a popular go-to Italian cocktail. The service is superb from start to finish, and it's not uncommon to get a tableside visit from Maria herself, who greets guests in the couple's restaurants as family.

Fiola Mare
3050 K St. NW, Ste. 101, 202-525-1402
fiolamaredc.com
Metro: Foggy Bottom-GWU (Orange, Silver, Blue Lines)

LEARN HOW TO BAKE
AT MILK BAR

Sugar-obsessed baker Christina Tosi may have opened her first Milk Bar in New York City, but she's a Washington, DC, girl at heart. Tosi grew up in suburban Northern Virginia, just outside of DC, and after earning her baking cred in NYC, she set her sights on DC. The bakery chain—famous for its addictive Crack Pie®, Compost Cookies®, B'Day Truffles, and more—now has three locations in DC. Her most recent opening in Logan Circle serves as the brand's DC flagship and features dine-in seating, an outdoor courtyard, and a baking classroom. Fans can take classes there (if you're lucky, you can even take a class from Tosi herself when she's in town), including an in-demand how-to on making Milk Bar's signature Crack Pie®. Sign up and see if you can replicate the sweet treat. Your newfound skills are sure to be a hit the next time you host a dinner party!

Milk Bar
1525 Fifteenth St. NW, 855-333-MILK (6455) (ext. 14)
milkbarstore.com

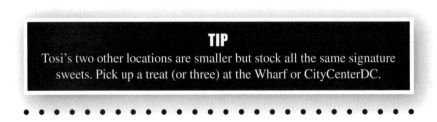

TIP
Tosi's two other locations are smaller but stock all the same signature sweets. Pick up a treat (or three) at the Wharf or CityCenterDC.

GET A TASTE OF THE AMALFI COAST
AT AN ARTISANAL LIQUEUR DISTILLERY

The tasting room for Don Ciccio & Figli is located in a fairly nondescript building in northwest DC, but follow the mermaids painted on the wall to the second floor and you'll enter a tiny corner of the Amalfi Coast. It's here that owner Francesco Amodeo painstakingly crafts small batch artisanal liqueurs using more than one-hundred-year-old recipes passed down from his grandfathers. The family recipes, the traditional Italian distilling methods, and the all-natural ingredients make for authentic liqueurs—from classic limoncello to more daring flavors, such as concerto (that would be espresso and barley)—perfect for sipping or mixing with cocktails. Amodeo opens his tasting room every Saturday from 1:00 to 6:00 p.m. for fans to get a glimpse behind the Amalfi curtain, but thanks to the runaway popularity of his liqueurs, more than twenty-five local restaurants also serve the brand at their bars. Try Lupo Verde, Rose's Luxury, Masseria, or Iron Gate to name just a few, to get a taste of, as the Italians say, "la dolce vita."

Don Ciccio & Figli
6031 Kansas Ave. NW
donciccioefigli.com

DC DISTILLERIES

Try these distillery and bar combos for some sipping and sampling around town:

District Distilling Co.
1414–1418 U St. NW
202-629-3787
district-distilling.com

New Columbia Distillers
1832 Fenwick St. NE
202-733-1710
greenhatgin.com

Founding Spirits at Farmers & Distillers
600 Massachusetts Ave. NW
202-798-6007
foundingspirits.com

One Eight Distilling
1135 Okie St. NE
202-636-ONE8
oneeightdistilling.com

Cotton & Reed
1330 Fifth St. NE
202-544-2805
cottonandreed.com

TIP

Want to take a taste of Italy home with you?
You can pick up Don Ciccio & Figli spirits in
a number of local liquor stores.

DINE YOUR WAY DOWN
THE FOURTEENTH STREET CORRIDOR

One of the District's most thriving neighborhoods is the Fourteenth Street Corridor with its mix of restaurants, retail, and residential. Also known as Logan Circle, the neighborhood has developed in the last decade to become a dining destination among locals. A mix of made-in-DC haunts and celebrity chefs offer something for every culinary taste. Stephen Starr's Le Diplomate is a smash hit among DC's social set with its French food and Paris bistro vibe, while Birch & Barley, one of Logan Circle's original restaurants, offers a head-spinning selection of 555 carefully curated beers. Try Doi Moi for Southeast Asian cuisine or Etto for Neopolitan pizzas served straight out of a brick oven. Or head to Pearl Dive Oyster Palace for some fresh seafood—and a round of bocce ball on its rooftop deck. Or simply set out and see which restaurant piques your interest as you make your way down Fourteenth Street.

TIP
Browse through local shop Salt & Sundry in between restaurant hopping. The homegrown store stocks a fabulous selection of home decor and entertaining items.

FOURTEENTH STREET EATS

Le Diplomate
1601 Fourteenth St. NW, 202-332-3333
lediplomatedc.com

Birch & Barley
1337 Fourteenth St. NW, 202-567-2576
birchandbarley.com

Doi Moi
1800 Fourteenth St. NW, 202-733-5131
doimoidc.com

Etto
1541 Fourteenth St. NW, 202-232-0920
ettodc.com

Pearl Dive Oyster Palace
1612 Fourteenth St. NW, 202-319-1612
pearldivedc.com

GET CREATIVE WITH YOUR FOOD
AT MINIBAR

Long before the nation's capital was considered an all-star foodie city, José Andrés, the godfather of dining in DC, was here making his culinary mark. In fact, it's fair to say that Andrés had an important role in putting the city on the gourmet map. Today, the all-star chef has sixteen restaurants in DC, but it's one of his originals—minibar—that remains the most in demand. The two-star Michelin restaurant is more fantastical food lab than traditional dining room, serving up avant-garde dishes and cocktails in a chef's table setting. It remains one of the hottest tickets in town, with tickets released two calendar months at a time, starting on the first Monday of each month. But with a capacity of just six diners per seating and a tasting menu that you'll talk about for years, this bucket list item is worth the wait.

minibar by José Andrés
855 E St. NW, 202-393-0812
minibarbyjoseandres.com
Metro: Gallery Place-Chinatown (Red, Yellow, Green Lines)

TIP
barmini, José Andrés's equally creative cocktail bar, is located next door.

HELLO, JOSÉ

Want a taste without the wait? Try one of these José Andrés restaurants with easier-to-get reservations:

Jaleo
480 Seventh St. NW
202-628-7949
jaleo.com

Zaytinya
701 Ninth St. NW
202-638-0800
zaytinya.com

Oyamel Cocina Mexicano
401 Seventh St. NW
202-628-1005
oyamel.com

China Chilcano
418 Seventh St. NW
202-783-0941
chinachilcano.com

America Eats Tavern
3139 M St. NW
202-450-6862
americaeatstavern.com

Beefsteak
Multiple locations in DC
beefsteakveggies.com

Fish by José Andrés
MGM National Harbor
101 MGM National Ave.
Oxon Hill, Maryland
301-971-6050
mgmnationalharbor.com/en/restaurants/fish-by-jose-andres.html

DINE AL FRESCO
WITH 4,500 OF YOUR CLOSEST FRIENDS

Consider it a flash mob for foodies. Le Dîner en Blanc, the outdoor dining experience that originated in Paris three decades ago, brings together thousands of diners in DC for a summer evening of revelry. The twist? Participants don't know the location until minutes before the event commences. Once it's announced, diners descend on the venue, dressed in all white to create the picture-perfect picnic experience. Participants must bring their own food, tables and chairs, white tablecloth, dinnerware, and, of course, champagne. The ceremonial waving of the napkins kicks off the unique event, and revelers light sparklers to signal the end of the meal. Previous DC dinner locations have included Pennsylvania Avenue with a view of the U.S. Capitol and in front of the Lincoln Memorial. Start shopping now for the perfect all-white outfit and mapping out your portable menu.

Le Dîner en Blanc
washington.dinerenblanc.com

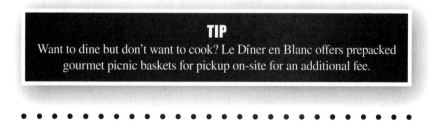

TIP
Want to dine but don't want to cook? Le Dîner en Blanc offers prepacked gourmet picnic baskets for pickup on-site for an additional fee.

HAVE DINNER
IN A COZY GEORGETOWN HOME

If you're looking for a quintessential Georgetown dining experience, make a reservation at 1789. Nestled inside a Federal-period home just outside the Georgetown University campus, this classic restaurant takes its name from the year the Constitution was ratified (which also happens to be the year Georgetown was founded) and reflects that eighteenth-century American atmosphere in its decor. Six separate dining rooms are all decorated to reflect the Federal-era style (think claw-footed mahogany furniture, eagle accents, and fox and hound hunting prints), while the hearty menu features seasonal farm-to-table fare such as rack of lamb, beef tenderloin, or lighter fish selections. A recently added bar and lounge are the perfect addition for a night cap. Washingtonians know it's a go-to for special occasion dining—or a simple weeknight meal for nearby neighbors.

1789
1226 Thirty-Sixth St. NW, 202-965-1789
1789restaurant.com

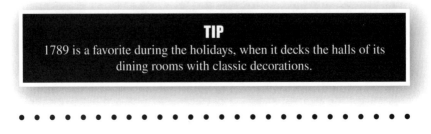

TIP
1789 is a favorite during the holidays, when it decks the halls of its dining rooms with classic decorations.

PUT YOUR PINKY UP
AT THE WILLARD

Spend an afternoon partaking in afternoon tea service at the Willard InterContinental. The two-hundred-year-old historic hotel hosts the time-honored tradition most weekends throughout the year, and it offers a wonderful way to experience the storied hotel. Lilting harp music sets the stage for tea, which is served in the Willard's Peacock Alley—an ornate hallway just off the hotel's lobby. A selection of teas, finger sandwiches, and pastries, including traditional scones, are served on fine china. During cherry blossom season, a Japanese-themed tea service is offered as part of the festivities. The winter holidays are a particularly lovely time to sit for tea. The hotel is decked out in its holiday finest, and seasonally inspired pastries are served as part of the tea service.

The Willard InterContinental Hotel
1401 Pennsylvania Ave. NW, 202-628-9100
washington.intercontinental.com
Metro: Metro Center (Red, Orange, Blue Lines)

TIP
Looking for something a bit less fussy? Have a drink in the Round Robin Bar, a popular and historic watering hole for DC's politicos.

TEA TIME!

A few more sophisticated spots for tea service:

Tea Cellar at Park Hyatt

1201 Twenty-Fourth St. NW
202-419-6755
hyatt.com/en-US/hotel/washington-dc/park-hyatt-washington-dc/wasph/dining

Empress Lounge at Mandarin Oriental

1330 Maryland Ave. SW
202-554-8588
mandarinoriental.com/washington/national-mall/luxury-hotel

The St. Regis Washington, D.C.

923 Sixteenth and K Sts. NW
202-509-8000
stregiswashingtondc.com

SAMPLE SOME SUDS
AT THE BREWMASTER'S CASTLE

Dupont Circle was once home to the wealthiest Washingtonians, but today very few of the neighborhood's turn-of-the-last-century homes remain. At least one mansion, though, the Heurich House, still stands tall on New Hampshire Avenue and is open to the public as a prime example of Dupont Circle's heyday. Also known as "The Brewmaster's Castle," the thirty-one-room mansion was home to Christian Heurich and his family from 1894 through 1956. Heurich made his name and his wealth as DC's most successful brewer. In a nod to his industry, visitors to the home today can take a guided tour that pairs information about the impressive interiors with a beer tasting. Beer samples are served as you walk through the house, and by the end of the tour, you've tried a full flight of local craft beers!

Heurich House Museum
1307 New Hampshire Ave. NW, 202-429-1894
heurichhouse.org
Metro: Dupont Circle (Red Line)

TIP
The Castle Garden at Heurich House is open to the public
Monday–Friday, 9:00 a.m. to 5:00 p.m.

SELECT FRESH SEAFOOD
AT THE HISTORIC FISH MARKET

Forget the grocery store. The best place to find fresh seafood in DC is at the Municipal Fish Market in southwest DC. Opened in 1805, it's the longest continuously operating open-air fish market in the United States, so it's no surprise that the vendors there know their seafood. Such vendors as Jessie Taylor Seafood and Captain White's Seafood City have been in business for multiple generations and can serve up seafood with a side of expertise. Fish fans will find a plethora of fresh options, ranging from whole Chesapeake blue crabs to prepared fish fillets. Make your selections for later or you can ask to have them prepped and served right there. Some vendors will even steam your crabs and shrimp on-site.

Municipal Fish Market
1100 Maine Ave. SW
wharfdc.com/fish-market/
Metro: Waterfront (Green Line) or L'Enfant Plaza (Orange, Silver, Blue, Yellow, Green Lines)

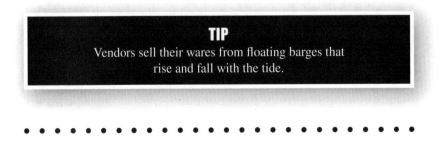

TIP
Vendors sell their wares from floating barges that rise and fall with the tide.

Courtesy of Gaylord National Resort

MUSIC AND ENTERTAINMENT

PACK A PICNIC
AND ENJOY THE SOUNDS OF SUMMER AT WOLF TRAP

Washingtonians know that a sure sign of summer is when Wolf Trap releases its musical lineup for the season. Nestled just outside of DC in Vienna, Virginia, the performing arts venue is the perfect place to pack a picnic (including wine!), throw a blanket on the grassy slope, and take in a performance as the sun sets. Wolf Trap's two outdoor venues, Filene Center and the Children's Theatre-in-the-Woods, host more than a hundred performances between them during the summer. From radio-friendly headliners to niche acts to kid-friendly shows, there's something for everyone. A particularly popular ticket is the National Symphony Orchestra shows, when the Kennedy Center loans out its nearly one-hundred-person orchestra to accompany everything from a classic opera to the music of *Jaws*.

Wolf Trap National Park for the Performing Arts
1645 Trap Road, Vienna, Virginia
703-255-1900
wolftrap.org

TIP
While Wolf Trap is mainly known as a summertime venue, it does offer performances in other seasons as well. Check out shows at the intimate indoor venue, the Barns at Wolf Trap, from October to May.

BE ENCHANTED BY THE PINK PETALS
AT THE NATIONAL CHERRY BLOSSOM FESTIVAL

Once a year the nation's capital is awash in cotton candy–colored flowers for the National Cherry Blossom Festival. The world-famous festival dates back more than one hundred years to when the mayor of Tokyo gifted DC with three thousand cherry trees. Today, those trees ring the Tidal Basin, creating a truly enchanting scene when the flowers hit their peak bloom in spring. The festival has grown over the years and is now a citywide event, featuring live music and entertainment along the Tidal Basin, along with a number of activities throughout DC. Don't miss your chance to fly a kite on the National Mall at the Blossom Kite Festival, see pink fireworks light up the sky at Petalpalooza at the Wharf, or watch cherry blossom–themed floats make their way down Constitution Avenue as part of the festival's closing parade, plus many other blossom-themed events at museums, hotels, and restaurants during the four-week festival.

National Cherry Blossom Festival
nationalcherryblossomfestival.com

PUT YOUR HOLIDAYS ON ICE
AT THE GAYLORD NATIONAL

The holiday season in DC is a magical time. Twinkling lights, bedecked trees, and plenty of holiday-themed events take over the city from Thanksgiving through New Year's Eve, but if you want to see a truly showstopping holiday display, head out just beyond DC to National Harbor in Oxon Hill, Maryland. It's there you'll find ICE!, a magical, walk-through display of hand-carved ice sculptures located inside the Gaylord National Resort. ICE! has its roots in Harbin, China, where talented carvers create a miles-long city made of ice every winter. A team of these master carvers travels to DC each year to put its talents on display with carvings based on popular heartwarming holiday stories. Previous years have featured *How the Grinch Stole Christmas* and *Rudolph the Red-Nosed Reindeer*. With only a handful of Gaylord properties around the country, DC is one of the few places to catch this impressive holiday display.

Gaylord National Resort
201 Waterfront St., National Harbor, Maryland
301-965-4000
gaylordnationalharbor.com

A NATION'S CAPITAL CHRISTMAS

Put these events on your holiday wish list:

The National Christmas Tree Lighting
thenationaltree.org

Zoo Lights at the National Zoo
nationalzoo.si.edu/events/zoolights

Downtown Holiday Market in Penn Quarter
downtownholidaymarket.com

Holiday Boat Parade at the Wharf
wharfdc.com/upcoming-events/

The Nutcracker at the Kennedy Center
kennedy-center.org

A Christmas Carol at Ford's Theatre
fords.org

Season's Greenings at the United States Botanic Garden
usbg.gov/plan-your-holiday-visit

Scottish Christmas Walk Weekend in Old Town Alexandria
campagnacenter.org/scottishwalkweekend

TIP

National Harbor is worth the trip in any season. The family-friendly development sits on the banks of the Potomac River and offers fun year-round. Ride the giant Ferris wheel, browse the Peeps store, check out the massive *Alive* statue, or set sail on an Urban Pirates boating adventure.

SPEND A SUMMER EVENING
LISTENING TO JAZZ IN A SCULPTURE GARDEN

The National Gallery of Art's expansive collection couldn't be contained in just two buildings. In 1999, the museum unveiled a six-acre sculpture garden that displays oversized works of contemporary art. The meandering, peaceful park tucked away just off Constitution Avenue is home to eye-popping sculptures such as Claes Oldenburg and Coosje van Bruggen's *Typewriter Eraser*, Alexander Calder's *Cheval Rouge*, Roy Lichtenstein's *House I*, and Barry Flanagan's *Thinker on a Rock*. The twenty-plus statues are worth a visit any time of year, but in the summer months, the National Gallery sponsors a jazz series on Friday evenings. Bring a blanket and picnic, or pick up some food and wine in the on-site Parisian-style Pavilion Cafe, and take in a live band as the sun sets on the week.

National Gallery of Art
Between Third and Ninth Sts. along Constitution Ave. NW
202-737-4215
nga.gov
Metro: Archives-Navy Memorial-Penn Quarter (Yellow, Green Lines)

CONTEMPORARY COURTYARD

Visit the Hirshhorn's Sculpture Garden and Plaza for even more outdoor modern art.

Smithsonian Hirshhorn Museum and Sculpture Garden

Independence Ave. and Seventh St. SW
202-633-4674
Metro: Smithsonian (Orange, Silver, Blue Lines)

TIP

A large fountain sits at the center of the sculpture garden at the National Gallery of Art and serves as a great place to rest and recharge after touring the museum. In the winter, it's transformed into one of DC's most beloved ice skating rinks. See where else to ice-skate in the city on page 63.

CELEBRATE THE NATION'S BIRTHDAY
WITH FIREWORKS ON THE NATIONAL MALL

Yes, nearly every city in America celebrates the Fourth of July with fireworks, but there's nothing quite like watching the pyrotechnics for the U.S.A.'s birthday with the Capitol Dome and Washington Monument as your backdrop. The main event is the fireworks at dusk, set to the sounds of a live concert on the West Lawn of the Capitol. The concert typically includes an all-star lineup of performers (Aretha Franklin, Faith Hill, Steve Martin, and the cast of *Sesame Street* have all graced the stage in previous years, to name a few), with patriotic music by the National Symphony Orchestra and the United States Army Ceremonial Band. Thousands of locals and out-of-towners flock to the National Mall on July 4 to watch the display, so you'll want to come early to lock in your space on the grass. Take Metro in, bring a blanket and picnic basket, and be prepared to use a port-a-potty, but it's all worth it when the music of Tchaikovsky's *1812 Overture* swells as the red, white, and blue fireworks boom overhead.

nps.gov/subjects/nationalmall4th/index.htm
pbs.org/a-capitol-fourth/home/
Metro: Smithsonian (Orange, Silver, Blue Lines)

COME FACE TO FACE WITH BOND VILLAINS
AT THE SPY MUSEUM

The nation's capital is home to the Central Intelligence Agency, National Security Agency, and FBI, to name a few organizations that traffic in international espionage. In fact, DC is home to more spies than anywhere on the planet—and you can learn about how they operate under constant cloak and dagger at the Spy Museum. Permanent exhibits include *School for Spies*, which offers an in-depth look at the tools of the trade, and *Spies Among Us*, which pulls back the curtain on how spying influenced the outcome of World War II. The newest exhibit, *Exquisitely Evil: 50 Years of Bond Villains*, showcases the silver screen's most popular spy, James Bond. The exhibit highlights some of the film series' most villainous stars and, of course, how Bond defeated them. You'll either walk out of the Spy Museum wanting to sign up at the CIA—or realizing that things aren't always what they seem.

International Spy Museum
800 F St. NW, 202-393-7798
spymuseum.org
Metro: Gallery Place-Chinatown (Red, Green, Yellow Lines)

EXPERIENCE HIP-HOP CULTURE
AT THE KENNEDY CENTER

Sitting on the banks of the Potomac River, the John F. Kennedy Center for the Performing Arts is one of the nation's preeminent performing arts venues. It's home to the prestigious National Symphony Orchestra and the Washington National Opera. It hosts a diverse lineup of more than three thousand events a year, from touring Broadway musicals to ballet performances to free nightly performances on the Millennium Stage and everything in between. One of the Kennedy Center's newest initiatives is a wide-ranging hip-hop program that aims to bring the influence of this American musical genre to the stage. The initiative, helmed by a Hip Hop Culture Council comprising such performers and producers as Q-Tip, Questlove, Common, and MC Lyte, promises to add to the Kennedy Center's innovative lineup of hip-hop performances (Kendrick Lamar accompanied by the National Symphony Orchestra was already a hit), film screenings, festivals, and more.

John F. Kennedy Center for the Performing Arts
2700 F St. NW, 202-467-4600
kennedy-center.org
Metro: Foggy Bottom-GWU (Orange, Silver, Blue Lines)
A dedicated Kennedy Center shuttle picks up patrons at the Metro stop.

TIP

What's all that construction? The Kennedy Center is currently undergoing a large expansion, scheduled to open some time in 2019, that will bring new pavilions to the campus with space for studios, rehearsal rooms, education programs, simulcast and video presentations, and additional dining options and green spaces.

WATCH THOUSANDS OF MOTORCYCLES
CONVERGE ON CONSTITUTION AVENUE

Memorial Day weekend traditionally marks the start of summer with pool time and picnics, but in DC the holiday stays true to its roots with a number of events honoring America's fallen soldiers. Thousands of wreaths are laid at Arlington National Cemetery. A concert on the West Lawn of the Capitol pays tribute to military sacrifice, and the country's largest Memorial Day parade makes its way down Constitution Avenue. But it's the Rolling Thunder Motorcycle Rally, held annually the Sunday of Memorial Day weekend, that is the weekend's most distinctive event. Rolling Thunder is devoted to honoring the POWs and MIAs of America's wars and attracts more than nine hundred thousand participants and spectators. The riders start at the Pentagon and then travel over the Arlington Memorial Bridge into DC before riding down Constitution Avenue with spectators lining the streets in support. The parade is most definitely a sight to see at least once. Consider it the world's largest motorcycle gang for good.

rollingthunder1.com

GET YOUR GROOVE ON
AT A GO-GO CONCERT

The nation's capital lays claim to the get-up-and-dance musical genre known as go-go thanks to DC native son and "godfather of go-go" Chuck Brown. Inspired by the sounds of funk and soul, Brown's music launched a live music movement in DC that reached its heyday in the seventies and eighties. Brown and other go-go bands would play for hours at venues all over the city for throngs of fans who came to dance and feel the percussion-heavy music. Brown passed away in 2012, but a number of go-go bands live on. Rare Essence, a nine-member band that got its start back in 1976, is passing the genre on to the next generation with local shows at such venues as the Hamilton and U Street Music Hall. The band performed with Chuck Brown himself and is considered one of the heirs to his legacy. If a live music show is on your DC list, grooving to go-go is a must.

rareessence.com

TIP
Other local go-go bands include Trouble Funk, Mambo Sauce, Team Familiar, and Junkyard Band.

SEE AN OFFBEAT PLAY
AT WOOLLY MAMMOTH THEATRE COMPANY

The *New York Times* called Woolly Mammoth "Washington's most daring theatre company" in 1991, and it's fair to say the assessment still fits today. The intimate theater in Penn Quarter seats just 265 patrons, giving anyone who attends an up-close and personal experience with the company's daring performances. Because of its experimental spirit, Woolly is also a breeding ground for new works that go on to make their mark in prestigious theaters across the country and around the world. At the same time, Woolly works to ensure that the experience is affordable and accessible for all, offering pay-what-you-can tickets on select nights and post-show panels and discussions. Experiencing a play at Woolly is sure to ignite a conversation with fellow theatergoers that will continue long after the metaphorical curtain goes down.

Woolly Mammoth Theatre Company
641 D St. NW, 202-393-3939
woollymammoth.net
Metro: Archives-Navy Memorial-Penn Quarter (Yellow, Green Lines)

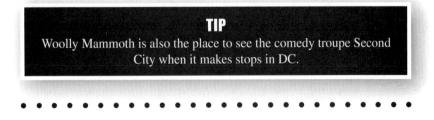

TIP
Woolly Mammoth is also the place to see the comedy troupe Second City when it makes stops in DC.

TAKE A BOW

Woolly Mammoth isn't the only theater in town to offer diverse and daring content. Grab tickets for a performance at these other DC-area stages:

Atlas Performing Arts Center
1333 H St. NE, 202-399-7993
atlasarts.org

Lincoln Theatre
1215 U St. NW, 202-888-0050
thelincolndc.com

Synetic Theater
1800 Bell St., Arlington, Virginia, 866-811-4111
synetictheater.org

Studio Theatre
1501 Fourteenth St. NW, 202-332-3300
studiotheatre.org

GALA Hispanic Theatre
3333 Fourteenth St. NW, 202-234-7174
galatheatre.org

WATCH AN ARMY BAND CONCERT
AT SUNSET

Summer weather and the fading sun serve as the backdrop to the Army's seasonal musical tradition known as Twilight Tattoo. On Wednesday evenings from April through August, audiences are welcomed onto Joint Base Myer–Henderson Hall in Arlington, Virginia, for an evening of military pageantry featuring soldiers from the Old Guard (3rd U.S. Infantry Regiment) and the U.S. Army Band "Pershing's Own," with performances from the U.S. Army Drill Team and the U.S. Army Blues, among other military musical talent. The free outdoor event features a mix of patriotic performances that offer a look at American military history set to music. Twilight Tattoo is a ceremonial tradition dating back to the Revolutionary War, when music was played to signal the end of the day and call soldiers back to their bunks. Today, it's a family-friendly tradition that locals look forward to every summer.

Twilight Tattoo
Joint Base Myer–Henderson Hall
Enter at Wright Gate
North Meade St. and Marshall Dr., Arlington, Virginia
202-685-2888
twilight.mdw.army.mil
Metro: Rosslyn (Orange, Silver, Blue Lines)

SUMMER SALUTES

Check out these other patriotic performances:

Concerts on the Avenue
navyband.navy.mil/cota.html

U.S. Military Band Summer Concert Series
aoc.gov/news/2018-military-bands-summer-concert-series

Sunset Parades
barracks.marines.mil/Parades/Sunset-Parade/

TIP

All adults will need a valid ID to enter Joint Base
Myer–Henderson Hall for Twilight Tattoo.

CELEBRATE SUMMER
AT THE NATIONAL BUILDING MUSEUM

The National Building Museum—with its soaring Corinthian columns, intricate friezes, and interactive architectural exhibits—is a must-visit year-round. But in the summer, the popular museum makes use of its cavernous Great Hall to host an always-buzzed-about artistic installation known as the Summer Block Party. In previous years, a "beach" took over the hall in the form of more than one million clear plastic balls (and yes, grown-ups *and* kids both dove in headfirst), a "bee hive" was constructed with 2,700 wound paper tubes, and visitors got lost in a larger-than-life maze. The 2019 installation is set to debut on July 4. No doubt this grand-scale art exhibition will be just as buzzy as in previous years.

National Building Museum
401 F St. NW, 202-272-2448
nbm.org
Metro: Judiciary Square (Red Line)

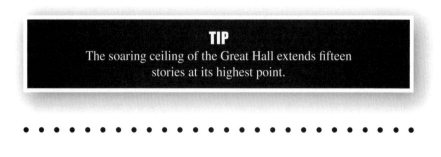

TIP
The soaring ceiling of the Great Hall extends fifteen stories at its highest point.

IMMERSE YOURSELF
IN AN EXPERIENTIAL ART GALLERY

Located next to a sandwich shop behind an easy-to-miss glass door, the exterior of ARTECHOUSE is unassuming, but step inside and this art-meets-technology gallery will transport you. Opened in 2017, the new gallery is devoted to installations that pair the power of interactive technology with art. The result is awe inspiring, and the rotating exhibits are sure to have you saying OMG. Take, for example, the multi-artist installation mounted during the 2018 cherry blossom season. Patrons stepped inside a darkened room surrounded by three oversized screens filled with whimsical cherry blossoms and koi fish—which came to life as visitors hovered their hands above the screens. Several other rooms also featured impressive interactive installations that brought the cherry blossoms to life. The gallery is unlike any other in DC right now, and the installations truly need to be seen to be believed.

ARTECHOUSE
1238 Maryland Ave. SW
dc.artechouse.com
Metro: Waterfront-SEU (Green Line)

TIP
Download ARTECHOUSE's app and then stop at the gallery's bar for an interactive cocktail. It's the only augmented reality cocktail bar in the country.

SWAY TO THE SOUNDS
OF JAZZ IN THE SUMMER

DC's jazz roots run deep. Native son Duke Ellington got his start here, playing in jazz clubs around the city—and DC's U Street District was a major hub for the genre during the height of its popularity, with venues hosting everyone from Ella Fitzgerald and Louis Armstrong to Lena Horne and Aretha Franklin. Every summer the city pays homage to its musical history with the DC Jazz Festival, an eleven-day citywide event that brings more than one hundred artists and acts to forty-plus venues across the region. The Howard Theatre, the Wharf, the Kennedy Center, and smaller neighborhood events are just some of the performances that fill up the festival calendar. The prestigious event features everyone from up-and-coming artists to Grammy Award–winning performers (for example, Leslie Odom Jr. of *Hamilton* fame was the headliner in 2018).

dcjazzfest.org

TIP
DC Jazz Fest features both free and ticketed events.

· ·

JAZZ IT UP

Catch some live jazz at one of these
venues throughout the year:

The Howard Theatre

620 T St. NW, 202-803-2899
thehowardtheatre.com

Blues Alley

1073 Wisconsin Ave. NW, 202-337-4141
bluesalley.com

Twins Jazz Club

1344 U St. NW, 202-234-0072
twinsjazz.com

Bethesda Blues and Jazz

7719 Wisconsin Ave., Bethesda, Maryland
240-330-4500
bethesdabluesjazz.com

KC Jazz Club at Kennedy Center

2700 F St. NW, 202-467-4600
kennedy-center.org

ROCK OUT
AT DC'S NEW WATERFRONT CONCERT HALL

In late 2017, the Wharf—a dazzling mile-long stretch of mixed-use waterfront real estate—was unveiled in southwest DC. The new area features a blend of restaurants, retailers, residences, and several live music venues. Anchoring the neighborhood's vibrant live music scene is the Anthem, an impressive space with state-of-the-art acoustics developed by the team behind DC's famous 9:30 Club. With seating that can accommodate anywhere from 2,500 to 6,000 people, the Anthem was designed to play host to both intimate performances and high-profile concerts. The Foo Fighters, led by Virginia native Dave Grohl, christened the venue as the opening act, and there's been a who's who of musicians on the lineup ever since. Instantly iconic, the Anthem is a must for any true live music lover.

The Anthem
901 Wharf St. SW, 202-888-0020
theanthemdc.com
Metro: Waterfront-SEU (Green Line),
L'Enfant Plaza (Orange, Silver, Blue, Yellow, Green Lines)

TIP
The Wharf is overflowing with waterfront restaurants and bars within walking distance of the Anthem. Stop in for a cocktail before or after the concert.

LIVE AND LOCAL

Snag tickets to a live music performance at
one of these local venues:

9:30 Club

815 V St. NW, 202-265-0930
930.com

Hamilton Live

1600 Fourteenth St. NW, 202-769-0122
live.thehamiltondc.com

Pearl Street Warehouse

33 Pearl St. SW, 202-380-9620
pearlstreetwarehouse.com

Union Stage

740 Water St. SW, 877-987-6487
unionstage.com

Black Cat

1811 Fourteenth St. NW, 202-667-4490
blackcatdc.com

GET SOME BELLY LAUGHS
AT THE BENTZEN BALL

DC isn't necessarily known as a comedy capital, but a ten-year-old festival is starting to change all that. Launched in 2009 by Brightest Young Things, an in-the-know digital magazine and event company, with comedian Tig Notaro, the four-day laugh fest attracts a who's who of comedians for stand-up performances and other events around town in October. Past performers have included Sarah Silverman, Jenny Slate, Jessica Williams, and Weird Al Yankovic. The 2018 lineup has a girl power theme, featuring a lineup of all women and non-binary headliners. It's also comedy with a conscience, with some ticket sales proceeds going to groups such as Planned Parenthood, the Human Rights Campaign, and Rock the Vote.

Bentzen Ball
brightestyoungthings.com/bentzen-ball

TIP
Try the DC Improv for stand-up comedy year-round.

EXPERIENCE THE POMP AND CIRCUMSTANCE
OF A PRESIDENTIAL INAUGURATION

The peaceful transfer of power is a hallmark of American democracy, and you can see it in action in Washington, DC. Every four years the nation's capital pulls out all the stops for the inauguration of the President of the United States. Whether welcoming a new president or starting a second term, the ceremony is a truly American experience. The swearing-in ceremony takes place outdoors at the U.S. Capitol, followed by a parade down Pennsylvania Avenue. You can request free tickets for the swearing-in ceremony through your senator or member of Congress, but most people generally bundle up (it's cold in DC in January!), hop on the Metro, and watch the ceremony and subsequent parade from public viewing areas.

Swearing-In Ceremony
U.S. Capitol, West Front Terrace
East Capitol and First Sts. SE
inaugural.senate.gov

TIP
Keep the party going at an "unofficial" inaugural ball. Many state societies and other groups hold inauguration parties. Tickets are usually much easier to score for these than the official balls the president attends.

STEP THROUGH THE SECRET DOORS
AT THE MANSION ON O STREET

From the outside, the Mansion on O Street is unassuming, but step inside and you'll be in a weird and wacky world that doesn't seem to quite fit with stoic Washington. The Mansion on O Street is actually a thirty-thousand-square-foot hotel and event space that stretches across five interconnected rowhouses. It's filled to the brim with all sorts of collectibles and oddities (and every last thing down to the studs is for sale). You can experience the mansion in a number of ways, such as booking one of the quirky themed rooms, having Sunday brunch, or attending an intimate musical performance, but probably the most popular way to experience this wild ride of a mansion is through the secret doors tour. More than seventy secret doors and passageways connect the five townhouses, and you can spend an afternoon poking around the house as you try to suss them out. Fair warning—the doors are indeed very well hidden, and the owners say if you can find even two you're a master sleuth! But it's still worth the price of admission . . . this one-of-a-kind mansion is truly a sight to behold.

The Mansion on O Street
2020 O St. NW, 202-496-2070
omansion.com
Metro: Dupont Circle (Red Line)

TEST YOUR LUCK
AT MGM NATIONAL HARBOR

Rising from the banks of the Potomac River in Prince George's County, Maryland, MGM National Harbor brought some Las Vegas glamour to the DC region when it opened its doors in 2016. The entertainment complex includes a vast 125,000-square-foot casino, a three-thousand-seat theater, high-profile restaurants helmed by such celeb chefs as José Andrés, and a sleek spa. Gamblers will love the twenty-four-hour casino floor with its 3,300 slot machines and 124 gaming tables. Just as in Vegas, however, you don't have to gamble to have fun. The MGM brand has attracted a who's who of headliners to the theater, including Bruno Mars, Britney Spears, Sting, and Cher. Sarah Jessica Parker has even gotten in on the act. The *Sex and the City* star opened her very first brick-and-mortar shoe store, SJP, inside the resort.

MGM National Harbor
101 MGM National Ave., Oxon Hill, Maryland
844-646-6847
mgmnationalharbor.com

TIP
The Atrium at MGM features a rotating display of eye-popping seasonal art installations that celebrate everything from the Christmas holidays to the Chinese Lunar New Year.

SPORTS AND RECREATION

SEE THE WORLD-FAMOUS GIANT PANDAS
AT THE SMITHSONIAN'S NATIONAL ZOO

A surefire hit among families, the Smithsonian's National Zoo is best known for its giant panda habitat, which is currently home to a family of three active pandas. The animals draw a crowd for their cute and cuddly factor, but the zoo is also home to one of the world's foremost conservation programs for the black-and-white bears. Visitors may find the popular pandas in their outdoor habitat or the indoor Panda House. They're not the only draw at the zoo, however. The California sea lions in the American Trail exhibit, orangutans in the Great Ape House, and Sumatran tigers in the Great Cats exhibit are just some of the more than 1,500 animals that call the National Zoo home.

Smithsonian's National Zoo
3001 Connecticut Ave. NW, 202-633-4888
nationalzoo.si.edu
Metro: Woodley Park-Zoo/Adams Morgan (Red Line)

TIP
Keep the party going with the zoo's popular Panda Cam. Panda fans can watch the bears play, eat, and sleep from two live cameras at nationalzoo.si.edu/webcams/panda-cam.

COOL OFF
IN THE CANAL BASIN AT CAPITOL RIVERFRONT

It's true that DC summers are known for their humid temperatures and sticky feel, but beyond retreating inside, locals have a few go-to places when summer temps are on the rise. One of the most delightful is Yards Park in the Capitol Riverfront neighborhood. This waterfront area stretches for nearly two miles along the lesser-known Anacostia River and offers an array of summertime fun. The Canal Basin, a wading pool that's just eleven inches deep, is the perfect respite for families with little ones. On sunny days, you'll find dozens of locals—children and adults alike—in shorts or swimsuits splashing in the water and sunning themselves on the surrounding grass. Dancing fountains sit atop the wading pool and also welcome little splashers looking to beat the heat. If you visit in the evening, the fountains add a rainbow of lights for a fun summery show.

Yards Park
355 Water St. SE
capitolriverfront.org/yards-park
Metro: Navy Yard-Ballpark (Green Line)

WATCH THE PRESIDENTS RACE
AT NATIONALS PARK

Is there anything more quintessentially American than watching America's favorite pastime *in* the nation's capital? After more than three decades without a baseball team, DC welcomed the Washington Nationals to town in 2005, and in 2008 they moved into their glittering, modern stadium in the shadow of the U.S. Capitol (in fact, select seats in the higher tiers offer a view of the Congressional building). Nats Park takes its federal history (not so) seriously with the fourth-inning Presidents Race. Oversized versions of George Washington, Thomas Jefferson, Abraham Lincoln, and Teddy Roosevelt take to the baseball field for a race to the delight of the crowd. Afterward, fans can grab a photo with the popular presidents at the top of Section 131. Out-of-towners may also want to use game day as an opportunity to sample some of the federal city's most famous food. The park has outposts of Ben's Chili Bowl, District Doughnut, and Dolci Gelati.

Nationals Park
1500 South Capitol St. SE
202-675-6287
mlb.com/nationals
Metro: Navy Yard-Ballpark (Green Line)

TRAVEL ALONG
ONE OF THE NATION'S MOST SCENIC ROADS

Both a parkway and a national park, the nearly twenty-five-mile stretch of road that makes up George Washington Memorial Parkway is arguably one of the most beautiful drives in America. The road hugs the Potomac River from Mount Vernon in Virginia to near Great Falls Park in Maryland. It's worth the leisurely drive to see it all, but the stretch that offers postcard views of DC's marble monuments and memorials is perhaps the most breathtaking. Just a few miles long, this portion of the drive is best seen by bicycle so you can stop along the way for photos. Start at Theodore Roosevelt Island and pedal your way on the bike trail past the Lincoln Memorial and Washington Monument, among others on the DC side, and the U.S. Marine Corps Memorial (also known as the Iwo Jima Memorial) and the Navy and Marine Memorial on the Virginia side. You'll pass Ronald Reagan Washington National Airport and end at Gravelly Point Park, which offers up-close views of planes taking off over the Potomac. On sunny days, you'll find locals crowding into this green patch to bike, picnic, and play pickup soccer in between marveling at the takeoffs and landings.

George Washington Memorial Parkway
nps.gov/gwmp

LACE UP YOUR SKATES
FOR A SCANDALOUS WASHINGTON EXPERIENCE

The Watergate Hotel will forever be synonymous with the Nixon presidential scandal, but after a recent multimillion-dollar facelift, the infamous hotel has entered a new era of luxury and once again serves as a social center in Washington, DC. In winter, one of its newest offerings is ice skating at the hotel's swanky rooftop bar and lounge, Top of the Gate (dubbed, cleverly, Top of the Skate). Head on up for a loop or two around the synthetic rink and take in the sweeping views of the city and across the river into Virginia. A skate-up bar with winter craft cocktails makes the scene at this rink primarily twenty-one-plus—but scandalous behavior isn't required to skate or sip. The hotel, which is situated conveniently close to the Kennedy Center, offers entertainment year-round. Book a room; dine at the hotel's main restaurant, Kingbird; or relax at the hotel's sophisticated spa, Argentta.

The Watergate Hotel
2650 Virginia Ave. NW, 202-827-1600
thewatergatehotel.com

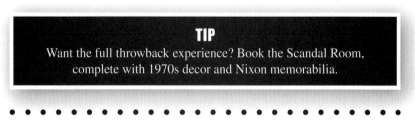

TIP
Want the full throwback experience? Book the Scandal Room, complete with 1970s decor and Nixon memorabilia.

GREAT SKATES

National Gallery of Art Sculpture Garden Ice Rink
Seventh St. and Constitution Ave. NW
nga.gov/visit/ice-rink.html

Washington Harbour Ice Rink
3000 K St. NW
thewashingtonharbour.com/skating

Fairmont Hotel Ice Rink
2401 M St. NW
fairmont.com/washington

The Wharf Ice Rink
Transit Pier
960 Wharf St. SW
wharfdc.com/wharf-ice-rink/

Canal Park Ice Rink
200 M St. SE
canalparkiceskating.com

COMPETE WITH SOLDIERS
IN THE MARINE CORPS MARATHON

Feeling patriotic? The Marine Corps Marathon descends on the District the last Sunday in October each year with more than twenty-seven thousand runners, including elite athletes from all branches of the military. Known as the "People's Marathon" because there's no qualifying event to participate (just a lottery to get into this wildly popular race), the event allows beginners to run shoulder-to-shoulder for 26.2 miles with servicemen and women. The race kicks off near the Pentagon and Arlington Cemetery with the presentation of colors, the singing of the National Anthem, and the blast of a M2A1 Howitzer cannon. Runners carrying full-sized American flags, wounded veterans, and Marines handing out medals at the finish line are just some of the touches that make this military-sponsored race stand out. A finish line festival rounds out the morning, with a beer garden, the Quantico Marine Corps Rock Band, and a photo opp in front of the Iwo Jima Memorial.

Marine Corps Marathon
marinemarathon.com

RACE TO THE FINISH LINE

Washington, DC's scenic monuments and memorials, plus its miles of trails, make it a popular spot for road races. Try these other running events throughout the year:

Rock 'n' Roll Marathon (March)
runrocknroll.com/dc

Cherry Blossom Ten-Miler (April)
cherryblossom.org

Parkway Classic (April)
runpacers.com/race/parkway-classic

Color Run (July)
thecolorrun.com/locations/washington-dc/

Army Ten-Miler (October)
armytenmiler.com

TIP

Registration for the Marine Corps Marathon happens in March. Spots fill up fast so be sure to sign up as soon as registration is available.

ASCEND THE EXORCIST STEPS...
IF YOU DARE

Most movies set in the nation's capital involve some sort of sweeping views of iconic memorials or walk-and-talks through the halls of the West Wing, but perhaps the most famous movie scene filmed here didn't involve any politics at all. The 1973 film *The Exorcist* includes that unsettling scene of Father Karras tumbling down a flight of steep stairs to his death after a successful exorcism. Those outdoor stairs weren't created on a Hollywood set. They're located in Georgetown and attract both movie buffs and exercise enthusiasts who want to conquer the seventy-five steps of fear. At any given time of day (or night), you'll see people making their way up and down the stairs, which sit just outside Georgetown University. A plaque notes their Tinseltown pedigree, and they're open for all to ascend or descend . . . whether it's night or day is up to you.

Exorcist Steps
3600 M St. NW
maps.georgetown.edu/exorciststeps
Metro: Foggy Bottom-GWU (Orange Silver, Blue Lines)

GET A NEW VIEW OF THE MEMORIALS
FROM THE WATER

If you walk the 2.1-mile loop of the Tidal Basin, a partially man-made body of water that sits between the Potomac River and the Washington Channel, you'll get photo-worthy views of both the Thomas Jefferson Memorial and the Washington Monument. Rent a pedal boat and you'll get an even cooler perspective. Trying out the pedal boats is fun all spring and summer, but make a note to rent one during cherry blossom season if you can to get the very best view. As home to the original gift of three thousand cherry trees, the Tidal Basin sits in the center of the action during the National Cherry Blossom Festival. Seeing the blooms from a pedal boat offers a truly spectacular way to experience the festival—and allows you to skip the crowds touring the trees from the Tidal Basin trail.

Pedal Boating at Tidal Basin
1501 Maine Ave. SW, 202-337-9642
boatingindc.com/boathouses/tidal-basin/

EXPLORE DC'S RIVERFRONT FUN
BY WATER TAXI

The DC region has plenty of riverfront real estate, and one of the best ways to see it all is by Potomac Riverboat Company's water taxi service. From the historic port-town feel of Old Town Alexandria to the preppy ambiance of Georgetown to fun-for-the-whole-family National Harbor to DC's newest waterfront neighborhood, the Wharf, you're going to want to hop off and explore these seaworthy destinations. You can pick up tickets at any of the piers and then enjoy a short ride between stops before debarking for some fun. Round-trip and one-way routes run from Georgetown, the Wharf, Old Town Alexandria, and National Harbor, which includes a stop at the Gaylord National Resort. There are even water taxis that will take monument watchers to the National Mall.

Potomac Riverboat Company
potomacriverboatco.com
703-684-0580

TIP
During baseball season, Potomac Riverboat Company offers a Baseball Boat cruise that takes fans from National Harbor and Old Town Alexandria to Nationals Park.

EXPLORE
ROCK CREEK PARK
ON HORSEBACK

For those looking for some green space in the city, Rock Creek Park offers an expansive 1,754-acre stretch of foliage-filled hiking and biking trails, picnic spaces, golfing, tennis, and other outdoor recreation. If you want to explore the picturesque trails on horseback, you can saddle up at the Rock Creek Horse Center. It's a unique way to get the lay of the land and find a peaceful retreat within the borders of DC. But with thirteen miles of trails throughout Rock Creek Park, there's more than one way to explore. Other than horseback, try one of the one- to ten-mile hiking loops—or simply unpack a picnic and dine beneath the canopy of trees. And speaking of looking up . . . Rock Creek is the only park in the National Park Service with a planetarium. Led by park rangers, many programs explore the night sky, even including outdoor star-gazing sessions.

Rock Creek Horse Center
Rock Creek Park, 5100 Glover Rd., 202-362-0117
rockcreekhorsecenter.com

TIP
Thompson Boat Center is also located inside Rock Creek Park
and offers rentals for kayaks, canoes, bicycles, and more.
(boatingindc.com)

SEE THE 2018 STANLEY
CUP CHAMPTIONS HIT THE ICE

Rock the red! Washington Capitals fans scored bragging rights to the Stanley Cup in the summer of 2018 when the hockey team finally went all the way—winning the NHL championship for the first time in the franchise's forty-four-year history. The Caps' home ice is at Capital One Arena in bustling Penn Quarter where bars and restaurants abound. Snag some tickets and watch Russian phenom Alex Ovechkin and his teammates whiz by on the rink. Follow it up with some bar hopping in Penn Quarter where you can talk shop with your fellow Caps fans. Plus, super fans may want to head to Kettler Capitals Iceplex in Arlington, Virginia. The Caps practice at a rink in the Ballston neighborhood and their ice time is open to the public. Stop by and see some of that Stanley Cup magic.

Capital One Arena
601 F St. NW, 202-628-3200
nhl.com/capitals
Metro: Gallery Place-Chinatown
(Red, Yellow, Green lines)

Kettler Capitals Iceplex
627 N. Glebe Road, Suite 800
Arlington, VA, 22203, 571-224-0555
kettlercapitalsiceplex.com
Metro: Ballston-MU (Orange, Silver lines)

TIP
Capital One Arena is also home to the the city's professional basketball teams: the Washington Wizards and Washington Mystics. If soccer is your sport, catch a DC United game at the brand new, twenty-thousand-seat Audi Field on the banks of the Anacostia River. Check out Audi Field's Fan Plaza with its live music, food and drink vendors, and other interactive experiences on game days.

PICNIC BENEATH THE CAPITOL COLUMNS
AT THE NATIONAL ARBORETUM

Although the U.S. National Arboretum is technically a research facility run by the United States Department of Agriculture, it's also one of the most gorgeous public gardens in the District. In spring and summer, the arboretum is bursting with color as its various plant and flower collections bloom. Look for azaleas, cherry blossoms, peonies, and boxwoods, among others, along with the National Grove of State Trees, which is home to trees representing every state and DC. Washingtonians know that the serene setting also makes the Arboretum a perfect place for a picnic. Lay out a blanket and unpack your basket in the shadow of the Capitol Columns. The twenty-two Corinthian columns are the originals from the U.S. Capitol but were replaced when the Capitol Dome needed additional support. Post-picnic, be sure to make time to explore the meandering grounds of this DC landmark.

National Arboretum
3501 New York Ave. NE, 202-245-2726
usna.usda.gov
Metro: Stadium-Armory (Orange, Blue Lines), transfer to Metrobus B2

GIDDY UP
ON A ONE-HUNDRED-YEAR-OLD CAROUSEL AT GLEN ECHO

A ride on a carousel that's been spinning for generations is a family tradition for many Washingtonians. Located just outside DC in suburban Maryland, Glen Echo Park opened in the 1890s as a retreat for city dwellers and—with the addition of an amphitheater, trolley, and amusement park rides and games—was a family-friendly spot for decades. Today, Glen Echo is a national park with a focus on the arts, but the carousel, installed in 1921 with hand-carved horses, still stands as the colorful centerpiece. A meticulous restoration of the classic carousel was completed in 2003, allowing a new generation of children to enjoy the enchanting ride. You'll also find other signs of eras past throughout the park, including the Spanish Ballroom and Bumper Car Pavilion (though now it's sans bumper cars). Weekly social dances in the Spanish Ballroom; a number of artist studios and galleries; and a children's theater, picnic space, café, and playground make Glen Echo a popular place year-round. But it's the carousel that continues to create a magical atmosphere for amusement park lovers of all ages.

Glen Echo Park
7300 MacArthur Blvd., Glen Echo, Maryland
301-634-2222
glenechopark.org

• •

FULL CIRCLE

Take a spin on these other local carousels:

National Carousel
(on the National Mall)
900 Jefferson Dr. SW
nationalcarousel.com

Conservation Carousel
National Zoo
3001 Connecticut Ave. NW
nationalzoo.si.edu/visit/attractions/carousel

The Carousel at National Harbor
137 National Plaza, National Harbor, Maryland 20745
nationalharbor.com/the-carousel/

TIP

The Glen Echo carousel operates between April and
September. Tickets are $1.25.

SEE THE CITY
BY SEGWAY

Why walk when you could Segway? There's a lot of ground to cover when touring the National Mall and surrounding monuments and museums. One of the best—and quirkiest—ways to see it all is by Segway. A number of tour companies offer guided tours on these futuristic-looking contraptions. You'll get a quick tutorial on how to steer the two-wheeled vehicles before suiting up with a helmet and heading out into the city. It can take a moment to find your balance, but once you've got it, you'll be zigging and zagging through DC's attractions in no time. Tour options include everything from the iconic monuments and memorials to stops at the many Smithsonian museums to seasonal tours during cherry blossom season. If you're a local, you may think this is a tour only tourists try, but when will you have another opportunity to test-drive a Segway?

City Segway Tours
citysegwaytours.com/washington-dc

Segs in the City
segsinthecity.com

Bike and Roll
bikeandrolldc.com

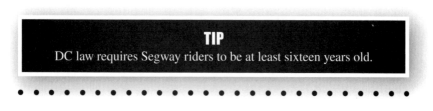

TIP
DC law requires Segway riders to be at least sixteen years old.

SPEND AN AFTERNOON
IN DC'S MOST SOCIAL CIRCLE

DC has many picturesque traffic circles, and you're sure to notice them if you're driving in the city. A number of them are large enough for socializing, but perhaps the most popular is Dupont Circle. The centerpiece is the intricate Dupont Circle fountain. In warmer months, you'll find all manner of locals and visitors alike congregating around it—some picnicking, others playing pickup chess, and even yogis and yoginis partaking in the occasional free yoga class held on the circle's large swath of grass. Pack a bag with a blanket, a book, and some sunblock and spend an afternoon sunning yourself with friends. The neighborhood's bevy of bars, restaurants, and retail shops means you can make a day of it.

washington.org/dc-neighborhoods/dupont-circle
Metro: Dupont Circle (Red Line)

TIP
Don't miss the Spanish Steps just a few blocks away.

• •

CULTURE AND HISTORY

GREET BARACK AND MICHELLE OBAMA
AT THE NATIONAL PORTRAIT GALLERY

What do Bill Gates, Michael Jackson, Queen Elizabeth, and Abraham Lincoln all have in common? Their likenesses hang in the National Portrait Gallery, a Smithsonian museum dedicated to telling the American story through paintings and photographs of individuals who have shaped the story of the nation. The museum offers a diversity of exhibits, from its *Presidential Portraits* permanent exhibition, which is the country's only complete collection of presidential portraits outside the White House, to contemporary images that capture today's pop culture zeitgeist. In early 2018, in a tradition that began with George H. W. Bush, the museum unveiled the official portraits of Barack and Michelle Obama, which are now part of the permanent collection. The modern portraits were painted by Kehinde Wiley and Amy Sherald, respectively, and are the first official presidential portraits painted by African American artists.

National Portrait Gallery
Eighth and F Sts. NW, 202-633-8300
npg.si.edu
Metro: Gallery Place-Chinatown (Red, Yellow, Green Lines)

TRAVEL BACK IN TIME
AT GEORGE WASHINGTON'S MOUNT VERNON

Washington, DC, is steeped in presidential history. From museums to monuments to restaurants, dozens of attractions pay tribute to the highest office in the land, but just outside DC in Alexandria, Virginia, is one of the most expansive presidential monuments. Mount Vernon was the home of America's first president, George Washington, and today it endures as a tribute to one of the nation's Founding Fathers. The estate consists of the mansion, along with a number of outbuildings and gardens and an interactive museum that all come together to paint a picture of life in Colonial America. Visitors can take a guided tour of the circa 1799 mansion, followed by free time to explore the rest of the estate, including Washington's Tomb, where George and Martha Washington are both buried. In the Museum and Education Center, kids will love the 4-D film that traces the Revolutionary War (complete with an indoor snowfall and vibrating seats!), and you can cap off your visit with a meal at the Mount Vernon Inn Restaurant, where servers in colonial garb take your order.

Mount Vernon
3200 Mount Vernon Memorial Hwy.
Mount Vernon, Virginia
703-780-2000
mountvernon.org

SEE THE MEMORIALS
AT THEIR MOST SPECTACULAR

Whatever your politics, one thing we can all agree on is that the nation's capital is an absolutely stunning city, and the monuments and memorials that stretch from the Lincoln Memorial to the U.S. Capitol are a breathtaking sight. These iconic structures are at their most spectacular at night. They are illuminated in the evenings for public viewing, giving them an even more dramatic quality than during daylight hours. You can tour them on your own on foot, but booking an organized tour is your best bet for viewing. Old Town Trolley Tours offers a Monuments by Moonlight tour that picks up at Union Station and makes the rounds to some of the most popular spots, including the World War II Memorial, FDR Memorial, Vietnam Veterans Memorial, Korean War Memorial, Martin Luther King, Jr. Memorial, and Lincoln Memorial.

Old Town Trolley Tours
(departs from Union Station)
50 Massachusetts Ave. NE, 202-832-9800
trolleytours.com/washington-dc
Metro: Union Station (Red Line)

TIP
Not only do after-dark tours offer a new view of DC's monuments and memorials, but in general, the attractions are also less crowded, giving you an even better view of these famous landmarks.

SEE THE WORLD'S MOST FAMOUS DIAMOND
AT THE NATURAL HISTORY MUSEUM

Rose's blue diamond in *Titanic* has nothing on the real thing. The film may have a storyline about a necklace that bears a striking resemblance to the world-famous Hope Diamond, but, thankfully, in real life, the Hope Diamond survived centuries of turmoil before finding a permanent home at the Smithsonian National Museum of Natural History. Its history dates back to 1668, when Marie Antoinette owned it before it changed hands and countries many times, ultimately finding its way to Harry Winston and eventually the Smithsonian. You can view the spectacular 45.5-carat diamond in the Hall of Geology, Gems, and Minerals, where a bevy of other gorgeous natural baubles are also on display. You'll want to make time for some of the museum's other permanent exhibits, including the fourteen-foot-tall African elephant that greets visitors in the rotunda, the forty-five-foot-long North Atlantic right whale (look up) in Sant Ocean Hall, and the live Butterfly Pavilion.

Smithsonian National Museum of Natural History
10th St. and Constitution Ave. NW, 202-633-1000
naturalhistory.si.edu
Metro: Smithsonian (Orange, Silver, Blue Lines)

READ THE COUNTRY'S FOUNDING DOCUMENTS
AT THE NATIONAL ARCHIVES

The guiding principles that reflect the American experiment are enshrined in the country's most important documents: the Declaration of Independence, the Constitution, and the Bill of Rights—and they're available for viewing at the National Archives. Housed in a beautiful neoclassical building along Pennsylvania Avenue, all three documents can be viewed in the Rotunda for the Charters of Freedom. Located beneath a soaring rotunda in the center of the building, the documents are encased in glass with low lighting and climate control—ensuring that visitors for generations to come can view the originals. The trio of founding documents aren't the only thing on display here. The National Archives is a working institution and includes thousands of additional records. In the Public Vaults, visitors can view an array of documents that tell America's story, including handwritten letters by George Washington, wartime telegrams from Abraham Lincoln, and presidential audio recordings from the Oval Office.

National Archives
700 Pennsylvania Ave. NW, 866-272-6272
archives.gov
Metro: Archives-Navy Memorial-Penn Quarter (Yellow, Green Lines)

OBSERVE ORAL ARGUMENTS
AT THE HIGHEST COURT IN THE LAND

The Supreme Court is where some of the most important legal decisions in this country's history are made—and visitors can vie for a seat to watch justice in action. Every year the nine justices that make up the bench hear arguments concerning one hundred to 150 cases between October and April. To observe, visitors must line up outside the courtroom the morning of a scheduled argument, and seats are given out on a first-come, first-served basis. It's not always as riveting as the legal dramas you see on television, but the constitutional impact lasts far longer than a season of *Law & Order*. If you visit the court on a day when no arguments are being heard, parts of the building are still open to the public, including several exhibitions about the court's history and courtroom lectures led by docents who explain how the third branch of government, the Judicial branch, operates.

U.S. Supreme Court
1 First St. NE, 202-479-3000
supremecourt.gov
Metro: Capitol South (Orange, Blue, Silver Lines), Union Station (Red Line)

VISIT ONE OF THE UNITED STATES'
GRANDEST TRAIN STATIONS

If you really want to see Union Station, look up. The train station is housed in a beautiful Beaux-Arts building constructed in 1907, but it's the ceiling that is arguably its most stunning architectural feature. Step inside the soaring ninety-six-foot-high room that serves as the gateway to the bustling train station and take in the gold leaf that runs the length of its expansive coffered ceiling in all directions. In 2011, an incredibly rare 5.8 earthquake shook Washington, DC, and damaged the historic ceiling. A five-year restoration, including regilding the ceiling with more than 120,000 sheets of twenty-three-karat gold, made it even more impressive. Listed on the National Register of Historic Places, Union Station is worth a tour stop even if you don't have a train to catch.

Union Station
50 Massachusetts Ave. NE, 202-289-1908
unionstationdc.com
Metro: Union Station (Red Line)

TIP
Union Station is DC's main hub for picking up tour transportation. The DC Ducks, Old Town Trolley Tours, Big Bus Tours, CitySights DC, Bike and Roll, and Grayline Tours all depart from here.

TRACE THE HISTORY
OF THE AFRICAN AMERICAN EXPERIENCE
AT THE SMITHSONIAN'S NEWEST MUSEUM

On September 24, 2016, then-President Barack Obama gave a stirring speech that officially unveiled the nineteenth Smithsonian museum. "It is a monument, no less than the others on this Mall, to the deep and abiding love for this country, and the ideals upon which it is founded," he told the assembled crowd. "For we, too, are America." The museum—wrapped in an intricate bronze metal lattice that recalls the ironwork crafted by enslaved African Americans—traces the history of the African American experience from the days of the slave trade dating back to 1400 through the tumult and triumphs of the modern era. Start in the History Galleries before making your way to the Community and Culture Galleries, which look at how the African American community has helped shape the story of modern America. The Contemplative Court, located on the third level of the History Galleries, features a ringed fountain of water raining into a pool from a skylight above and offers a reflective space within the museum.

Smithsonian National Museum of African American History and Culture
1400 Constitution Ave. NW, 844-750-3012
nmaahc.si.edu
Metro: Federal Triangle (Orange, Silver, Blue Lines),
Smithsonian (Orange, Silver, Blue Lines)

• •

TIP

Open for just over two years, the museum remains one of the hardest tickets in town to get. While free, visitors must obtain timed-entry passes, which are released for upcoming dates the first Wednesday of each month. Or, you can go online at 6:30 a.m. each morning to check if any same-day passes will be available. Walk-ups are welcome starting at 1:00 p.m. on weekdays, and veterans, active-duty personnel, and first responders may obtain walk-up passes at any time for themselves and one guest.

MARVEL
AT THE FRIENDSHIP ARCH IN CHINATOWN

DC's Chinatown is a blink-and-you'll-miss-it few blocks located within the larger bustling neighborhood of Penn Quarter, but despite its small size, the neighborhood still welcomes visitors with its colorful Friendship Arch. Built in 1986, the arch towers over a major intersection at Seventh & H Streets NW in downtown DC. Nearly sixty feet tall, the brightly colored archway features 272 dragons and seven pagodas at its peak. It's located near the city's biggest sports and entertainment venue, Capital One Arena, and is surrounded by a plethora of restaurants, bars, and museums, making it a happy surprise for anyone who comes upon it on their way to another attraction. While DC's Chinatown may be small, you can still find a handful of authentic hole-in-the-wall restaurants serving up dim sum, homemade noodles, and other traditional Chinese fare.

Metro: Gallery Place-Chinatown (Red, Yellow, Green Lines)

TIP
Chinatown has mostly been usurped by bustling Penn Quarter, but signs of its roots remain. Look for Chinese characters on the doors of each place of business in the neighborhood. DC law requires that all businesses display their names in Chinese.

TOUR THE PEOPLE'S HOUSE
AT 1600 PENNSYLVANIA AVENUE

It's the most famous house in America. You've seen it on television and in history books, but pictures simply don't do the White House justice. Whatever your politics, stepping inside offers a sense of history and patriotism. Touring the White House does take some advance planning, but if you can arrange to see it, it's absolutely worth your time. Public tours must be arranged through your member of Congress up to three months in advance and no less than twenty-one days in advance. What will you see on your self-guided tour? Visitors make their way through the East Wing, which includes the Blue, Red, and Green Rooms, as well as the State Dining Room, China Room, and a view of the White House Rose Garden. Make sure to include the White House Historical Association across the street as part of your tour, which includes more than a hundred presidential artifacts and in-depth exhibitions about the history of the White House.

The White House
1600 Pennsylvania Ave. NW, 202-456-7041
whitehouse.gov/about-the-white-house/tours-events/
Metro: Federal Triangle, McPherson Square (Orange, Silver, Blue Lines),
Metro Center (Red, Orange, Silver, Blue Lines)

LOOK UP
AT THE WORLD'S TALLEST OBELISK

A trip to the National Mall isn't complete without viewing the Washington Monument. Towering above the rest of the white marble monuments and memorials, the Washington Monument stands at just under 555 feet tall. It pays tribute to, of course, President George Washington. The design was modeled after the great obelisks in Egypt and was meant to signal the timelessness of the nation's very first leader. Stand at the base of the monument and look up to feel its full size or snap some photos from farther away to capture the complete structure. You may notice that the monument appears two-toned. That's not your eyes playing a trick on you. Construction of the monument was halted during the Civil War, and stones from two different quarries were used during the first and second phase.

Washington Monument
2 Fifteenth St. NW, 202-426-6841
nps.gov/wamo
Metro: Smithsonian (Orange, Silver, Blue Lines)

TIP
The Washington Monument is currently closed to modernize the elevator. It is scheduled to reopen to visitors in spring 2019. The 360-degree views of the city are definitely worth the ride to the top!

SEE THE KITCHEN
THAT INSPIRED AMERICANS TO COOK

The Smithsonian is often referred to as "America's attic," and no doubt the best example of this is the Smithsonian's American History Museum. The collection here traces American history from the serious to the silly. Look for everything from the famous American flag that inspired Francis Scott Key to pen the National Anthem to Jim Henson's funny Swedish Chef Muppet. But one of the most popular stops in the museum is Julia Child's Cambridge, Massachusetts, kitchen. The culinary queen taped her popular PBS cooking show here for many years, and it's fully stocked with her trusty tools and pots and pans from the 1940s through 2001. Peek through the glass and picture yourself stirring a pot while sipping a glass of wine with Julia herself. The kitchen is located in the permanent exhibition *FOOD: Transforming the American Table 1950–2000*, which looks at fifty years of food in America, from farming to fast food.

Smithsonian National Museum of American History
1300 Constitution Ave. NW, 202-633-1000
americanhistory.si.edu
Metro: Smithsonian (Orange, Blue, Silver Lines)

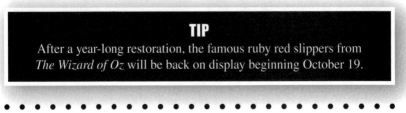

TIP
After a year-long restoration, the famous ruby red slippers from *The Wizard of Oz* will be back on display beginning October 19.

ROLL OUT YOUR SLEEPING BAG
AT THE SMITHSONIAN

In the 2009 movie *Night at the Museum: Battle of the Smithsonian*, Ben Stiller goes on an after-hours adventure through the Smithsonian museums as the exhibits come to life. Families can get their own version of this adventure with a Smithsonian Sleepover. Available at the American History Museum, Natural History Museum, and the Udvar-Hazy Center out in Virginia, the event invites kids (and their parents) for an evening of educational fun, followed by sleeping under some of the Smithsonian's most famous exhibits. At the Natural History Museum, for example, you'll slumber in Sant Ocean Hall beneath a suspended forty-five-foot-long North Atlantic right whale replica. Sleepovers take place on Friday nights in the summer months—the perfect finale to a day exploring the world-famous museums.

Smithsonian Sleepovers
smithsoniansleepovers.org

TIP
Don't have kids but still think a Smithsonian Sleepover sounds like a good idea? The Smithsonian's National Zoo offers twenty-one-plus sleepovers. Sleep in a tent on Lion/Tiger Hill, get a guided tour from a zookeeper, and enjoy wine and cheese before bedtime.

SNAP A PHOTO
WITH THE MOST FAMOUS DOG IN WASHINGTON

Presidential legend has it Harry Truman once said, "If you want a friend in Washington, get a dog." Perhaps he was thinking of his presidential predecessor, Franklin Delano Roosevelt, and his First Pooch when he expressed this sentiment. FDR's Scottish terrier, Fala, often accompanied the thirty-second president and was even known to do tricks. He was such a famous presidential pet that he's enshrined within the Franklin Delano Roosevelt Memorial. The sweet statue is a popular photo opp for visitors, but, of course, the memorial pays tribute to FDR's unprecedented four-term presidency in a more serious manner as well. Located along the Tidal Basin, the memorial was designed with four outdoor "rooms" tracing the Commander-in-Chief's administration from the Great Depression through the New Deal through World War II. Bronze sculptures, FDR's own words engraved in the marble walls, and small waterfalls create a space that allows for quiet reflection. It's one of the most original presidential memorials, and absolutely worth a spot on your sightseeing list.

FDR Memorial
1850 West Basin Dr. SW, 202-426-6841
nps.gov/frde
Metro: Smithsonian (Orange, Silver, Blue Lines)

EXPLORE THE ELEGANT ESTATE
OF AN HEIRESS

Post Cereal heiress Marjorie Merriweather Post spent years as a serious art collector, demonstrating a passion for the French decorative arts as well as works from pre-Revolutionary Russia. In fact, she amassed the largest collection of Imperial Russian art outside the country itself. You can view her life's work at her Georgian-style mansion-turned-museum, Hillwood Estate, which has been perfectly preserved to showcase what life was like for a socialite in the mid-twentieth century. From china to jewelry to furniture to paintings, her belongings are carefully curated and displayed in the seventeen main rooms. Don't miss her Fabergé collection, which includes nearly ninety pieces, most of which are on display in the Icon Room. Post purchased two Fabergé eggs during her trips abroad, and her seal of approval for the jeweler helped it become the sought-after brand that it is today.

Hillwood Estate, Museum & Gardens
4155 Linnean Ave. NW
202-686-5807
hillwoodmuseum.org
Metro: Van Ness-UDC (Red Line); it's a one-mile walk to Hillwood

GLORIOUS GARDENS

These historic homes also boast tour-worthy gardens:

Tudor Place
1644 Thirty-First St. NW
202-965-0400
tudorplace.org

Dumbarton Oaks
1703 32nd St. NW
202-339-6400
doaks.org

TIP

Don't miss the twenty-five acres of meticulously manicured gardens at Hillwood. Visitors are invited to bring their own picnics (or purchase food and drink in the café) and spend time luxuriating among the flowers.

CLIMB INTO EINSTEIN'S LAP
ON CONSTITUTION AVENUE

You don't have to be a science buff to make a stop at the Albert Einstein Memorial. The family-friendly bronze statue sits in an elm and holly grove on the grounds of the National Academy of Sciences and pays tribute to the world's most renowned scientist. It depicts the physicist sitting on a bench holding a paper with mathematical equations, including the Theory of General Relativity, with some of his most inspiring quotes engraved on the bench. The statue was erected to celebrate what would have been Einstein's one hundredth birthday in 1979 and celebrates its fortieth year welcoming visitors in 2019. While Einstein's work was groundbreaking, the memorial appears somewhat relaxed, with Einstein seated in a casual position. In fact, on many days, you'll find children turning the twenty-one-foot-tall memorial into a playground and climbing into Einstein's lap!

Albert Einstein Memorial
2101 Constitution Ave. NW
Metro: Foggy Bottom-GWU (Orange, Silver, Blue Lines)

TIP
The sculptor, Robert Berks, was known for his busts. He also sculpted the John F. Kennedy bust that sits in the Grand Foyer at the Kennedy Center.

WATCH THE SUNRISE
FROM THE LINCOLN MEMORIAL

The Lincoln Memorial is one of the National Mall's most moving memorials any time of day. The sixteenth president is enshrined in marble, sitting at an imposing nineteen feet tall, with the stirring words of two of his most famous speeches—the Gettysburg Address and his Second Inaugural—etched into the walls on either side of him. As one of the most popular monuments in DC, the Lincoln Memorial draws nonstop crowds of people who want to look up and marvel throughout the day. If you want to see the statue with a little more peace and quiet, try arriving when it was meant to be seen—at sunrise. Lincoln faces east, steadfastly looking out over the Reflecting Pool and past it to the Washington Monument. Sit on the steps of the Lincoln Memorial and watch the sun ascend with the Washington Monument as the backdrop. It's a stunning scene worthy of setting your alarm clock extra early.

Lincoln Memorial
2 Lincoln Memorial Cir. NW, 202-426-6841
nps.gov/linc
Metro: Foggy Bottom-GWU (Orange, Silver, Blue Lines)

STAND FOR THE CHANGING OF THE GUARD
AT ARLINGTON NATIONAL CEMETERY

Arlington National Cemetery serves as the official resting place for the nation's service men and women. With more than four hundred thousand uniform headstones in seemingly endless rows and an average of nearly forty military funerals per week, it's hallowed ground. The Tomb of the Unknown Soldier, which honors unidentified fallen soldiers, is where the solemn Changing of the Guard ceremony takes place. A soldier from the U.S. Third Infantry Regiment stands sentry over the Tomb of the Unknown Soldier day and night. The regimented ceremony involves a white glove inspection of the sentinel's rifle and precision marching that ensures the Tomb is never without a guard. Visitors have the privilege of watching when the cemetery is open, but the ceremony takes place even after hours, no matter the weather, serving as a stark reminder of what the nation's soldiers sacrificed in combat.

Arlington National Cemetery
1 Memorial Ave., Arlington, Virginia, 877-907-8585
arlingtoncemetery.mil
Metro: Arlington Cemetery (Blue Line)

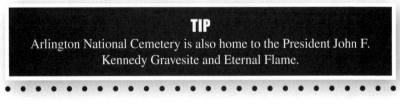

TIP
Arlington National Cemetery is also home to the President John F. Kennedy Gravesite and Eternal Flame.

LOOK UP
AT THE NATIONAL AIR AND SPACE MUSEUM

There's a reason they call it the "final frontier." Man's fascination with aviation and space exploration has endured since Galileo first peered at the sky through his telescope in the early seventeenth century through today as the Elon Musks of the world look to put a man on Mars. At the Smithsonian National Air and Space Museum, which is, unsurprisingly, one of the most popular museums in the world, visitors can trace the rich history of both aviation and space travel. The museum offers twenty-two in-depth exhibition galleries plus a planetarium, observatory, and IMAX theater, but before you set out to explore them all, you'll want to take in what's above you as you first step through the entrance. The Boeing Milestones of Flight Hall is an awe-inspiring trip through aeronautical history with famous aircraft, from the *Spirit of St. Louis* to the Lunar Module LM-2, all suspended above. You can even touch a volcanic rock brought back from the final moon landing in 1972. It sets the scene for the rest of your visit—and reminds you just how far man has come in his quest to understand the universe.

Smithsonian National Air and Space Museum
Independence Ave. and Sixth St. SW, 202-633-2214
airandspace.si.edu
Metro: L'Enfant Plaza (Orange, Silver, Blue, Yellow, Green Lines)

• •

FIND DARTH VADER
AMONG THE NATIONAL CATHEDRAL'S GARGOYLES

The National Cathedral in Northwest DC is a neo-Gothic feat of architecture that recalls the centuries-old cathedrals common throughout Old World Europe. From its stunning stained glass, soaring columns, and flying buttresses all the way down to its intricately carved gargoyles and grotesques that peek out from their perches on the exterior, the National Cathedral has served as the backdrop for a number of presidential state funerals and memorial services as well as post-Inauguration Day national prayer services. All are welcome at the daily Episcopal services, but many visitors choose a more in-depth tour to explore this landmark. One of the most popular? The seasonal (May–September) gargoyles guided tour. Bring your binoculars to spot the two hundred-plus carvings, and don't leave without looking for the famous Darth Vader gargoyle, which was added in the 1980s as part of a design contest for children. Also added as a result of that contest? A raccoon and a girl with pigtails and braces.

Washington National Cathedral
3101 Wisconsin Ave. NW, 202-537-6200
cathedral.org
Metro: Cleveland Park (Red Line); it's just under a mile walk to the Cathedral

SPOTLIGHT ON SANCTUARIES

These religious centers are also worth a visit:

National Shrine of the Immaculate Conception

400 Michigan Ave. NE
202-526-8300
nationalshrine.com

Franciscan Monastery

1400 Quincy St. NE
202-526-6800
franciscan.org

Sixth & I Synagogue

600 I St. NW
202-408-3100
sixthandi.org

TIP

Want an even closer look at the gargoyles? Opt
for the year-round Tower Climb tour, which
gives you access to the Bell Tower and a
no-binoculars-needed look at the gargoyles on the
west tower, both by a steep stair climb.

STAND IN STATUARY HALL
FOR AN EAVESDROP SESSION

Touring the U.S. Capitol offers an up-close look at the business of government. The building—a central domed rotunda flanked by the House and Senate chambers—is home to the congressional branch of government and attracts millions of visitors to its hallowed halls each year. You'll start in the underground interactive visitors center with an introductory film. Free ninety-minute tours take you through the history of U.S. government with a look at several key rooms, including the Capitol dome (look up to see the *Apotheosis of Washington* mural painted by Constantino Brumidi in 1865) and the Crypt (stand on the star that denotes the very center of Washington, DC). National Statuary Hall is always a hit for both its busts of famous figures and its parlor trick. Your guide should point out the right place to stand for "eavesdropping." Based on the curvature of the domed room, you can hear even whispered conversations from across the room. Be careful not to divulge any state secrets!

U.S. Capitol Visitor Center
East Front Plaza
First and East Capitol Sts. NE, 202-226-8000
visitthecapitol.gov
Metro: Union Station (Red Line), Capitol South (Orange, Silver, Blue Lines), Federal Center SW (Orange, Silver, Blue Lines)

VISIT THE THEATER
WHERE ABRAHAM LINCOLN
WAS ASSASSINATED

The assassination of Abraham Lincoln was one of the darkest events in American history, but despite his untimely death, the sixteenth president created a lasting legacy that still reverberates today. Both Lincoln's legacy and assassination are explored at Ford's Theatre, which does double duty as a museum and a working theater. Visitors can take a self-guided tour of the theater, which has been preserved to look just as it did on April 14, 1865, including the presidential box where Lincoln was seated. A short lecture by a national park ranger provides a detailed account of that fateful evening and in the summer months, *One Destiny*, a thirty-minute play, is also presented as part of the tour. With tickets to the museum, you can trace the history of President Lincoln from his administration through the aftermath of the assassination. Be sure to reserve a ticket that also includes a look at the Petersen House, the boarding house across the street where Lincoln was taken following the shooting and later passed away.

Ford's Theatre
511 Tenth St. NW, 202-347-4833
fords.org
Metro: Metro Center (Red, Orange, Silver, Blue Lines),
Gallery Place-Chinatown (Red, Yellow, Green Lines)

PAY YOUR RESPECTS
AT THE VIETNAM VETERANS MEMORIAL

Amidst the white marble monuments and memorials on the National Mall stands a study in contrast. The Vietnam Veterans Memorial is a simple yet stunning piece of architecture that pays tribute to the fifty-eight thousand brave soldiers who died or were declared missing in action during the Vietnam War. The memorial consists of two black granite walls, each extending 246 feet and 9 inches, that contain rows upon rows of engraved names. While simple in its design, it's a powerful illustration of the human toll of war. Names are displayed in chronological order by date and time of casualty and can be found using an on-site reference book or visiting the Vietnam Veterans Memorial Fund's website. In the evening, the memorial, accessible twenty-four hours a day, takes on an even more dramatic feel with lighting that illuminates the wall. Whatever time you choose to visit, the mood is always hushed and respectful.

Vietnam Veterans Memorial
5 Henry Bacon Dr. NW
nps.gov/vive
Metro: L'Enfant Plaza (Yellow, Green Lines)

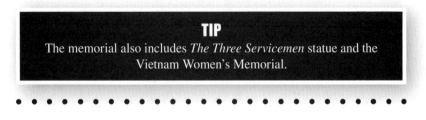

TIP
The memorial also includes *The Three Servicemen* statue and the Vietnam Women's Memorial.

MORE MILITARY AND WAR MEMORIALS

World War II Memorial
1750 Independence Ave. SW
nps.gov/wwii

Korean War Veterans Memorial
900 Ohio Dr. SW
nps.gov/kowa

African American Civil War Memorial
1925 Vermont Ave. NW (1st and U Sts.)
afroamcivilwar.org

DC World War I Memorial
West Potomac Park off Independence Ave. SW

U.S. Marine Corps War Memorial (Iwo Jima)
US Marine Memorial Cir., Arlington, Virginia
nps.gov/gwmp

Women in Military Service for America Memorial
Arlington National Cemetery, Arlington, Virginia
arlingtoncemetery.mil

United States Air Force Memorial
1 Air Force Memorial Dr., Arlington, Virginia
airforcememorial.org

United States Navy Memorial
701 Pennsylvania Ave. NW
navymemorial.org

FEEL LIKE A BUMBLEBEE
AT THE PHILLIPS COLLECTION

Credited as the country's first modern art museum, the Phillips Collection opened in 1921 and continues to add to its impressive collection of prestige contemporary works. In 2013 the Dupont Circle museum unveiled the Laib Wax Room. It's an installation that features, you guessed it, a wax room. German artist Wolfgang Laib, who is known for his use of organic substances found in nature, selected the Phillips to create his first permanent wax room after seeing the museum's Rothko Room, another avant-garde installation. Made from 882 pounds of beeswax that the artist collected himself, the sweet-smelling installation fills a small room and is illuminated by a single bare light bulb. Only one or two patrons may enter at a time, allowing for a contemplative experience.

The Phillips Collection
1600 Twenty-First St. NW, 202-387-2151
phillipscollection.org
Metro: Dupont Circle (Red Line)

TIP

The Phillips Collection is also home to a number of impressionist paintings, including Auguste Renoir's familiar *Luncheon of the Boating Party*.

CONTEMPLATE THE MEANING OF "NEVER AGAIN"
AT THE HOLOCAUST MUSEUM

The United States Holocaust Memorial Museum is not for the faint of heart. The museum is raw and unrelenting in its depiction of the horrors of the Holocaust—and it's also one of the most important museums in the world. A day spent here is something that everyone should do at least once—but prepare yourself for an emotional visit. The museum's permanent exhibition is spread among three floors and traces the era from the rise of Nazism to post-war liberation, offering a comprehensive view of this dark period in world history. But it's the artifacts of the victims that truly illustrate the human suffering. A simple but powerful display of four thousand shoes—everything from high heels to baby booties—that were seized from prisoners on their way to the Majdanek concentration camp paints a disturbing picture of the magnitude of victims. Finish your visit in the exhibition theater, where you can watch first-person Holocaust survivor testimonials.

United States Holocaust Memorial Museum
100 Raoul Wallenberg Place SW, 202-488-0400
ushmm.org
Metro: Smithsonian (Orange, Silver, Blue Lines)

SEE THE BERLIN WALL UP CLOSE
AT THE NEWSEUM

"Mr. Gorbachev, tear down this wall." So goes the famous line from President Ronald Reagan during the Cold War seen on front pages around the world. When the Berlin Wall did eventually tumble, the American news media was there, offering a front-row seat to history. Spread across six floors, the Newseum looks at such headline-making history through the lens of an ever-evolving news media. Start on the concourse level, where eight sections of the Berlin Wall are displayed (the largest piece of the Berlin Wall outside of Germany) along with an interactive gallery that tells the story of how news and information helped lead to the eventual fall of East Berlin. Plus, look for the new virtual reality feature that allows visitors to "walk" the streets of East Germany during the Cold War. From the Revolutionary War to September 11 and beyond, the Newseum takes visitors on a journey that highlights the importance of the First Amendment in American democracy.

Newseum
555 Pennsylvania Ave. NW, 202-292-6100
newseum.org
Metro: Archives-Navy Memorial-Penn Quarter (Yellow, Green Lines),
Judiciary Square (Red Line)

TAKE A SPIN AROUND THE GLOBE
WITHOUT LEAVING DC

As home to dozens of embassies, Washington, DC, is the epicenter of the diplomatic community, and every May more than seventy embassies throw open their doors as part of Cultural Tourism DC's Passport DC, a month-long celebration of food, art, dance, fashion, music, and more. Events are scheduled on each Saturday throughout the month, including the Around the World Embassy Tour, which welcomes visitors for an afternoon of interactive cultural demonstrations. The event is free, and participants can visit many embassies—a number of which are located within walking distance of each other along Massachusetts Avenue (on what's often referred to as Embassy Row) in the Kalorama neighborhood. The European Embassies Open House Tour focuses on the arts and culture of EU countries, while the Embassy Chef Challenge showcases the talents of embassy chefs through an evening of tastings. The Fiesta Asia! Street Festival and the International Children's Festival (held the last weekend in April) round out the programming.

Passport DC
culturaltourismdc.org

COMMUNE WITH FRIDA KAHLO
AT THE NATIONAL MUSEUM OF WOMEN IN THE ARTS

DC's National Museum of Women in the Arts holds the distinction of being the only major museum in the world dedicated solely to women artists. The museum boasts 4,500 works by more than one thousand artists spanning the artistic landscape from the sixteenth century through the present day. Many artists have a home here, including Frida Kahlo. Her painting *Self-Portrait Dedicated to Leon Trotsky* is an ode to her affair with the Russian revolutionary. It's also the only Frida Kahlo painting on permanent display in Washington, DC. Besides its permanent collection, the National Museum of Women in the Arts mounts ten exhibitions per year and supplements them with programming such as gallery talks, films, and even a chamber music series. The museum's gift shop is also considered one of the best in the city, offering everything from coffee table books to jewelry, all reflecting the museum's female-focused collection.

National Museum of Women in the Arts
1250 New York Ave. NW, 202-783-5000, nmwa.org
Metro: Metro Center (Red, Orange, Silver, Blue Lines)

SEE WHERE THE MONEY GETS MADE

Have you ever stopped to wonder how your money gets made? Those bills in your wallet are most likely produced in Washington, DC, at the Bureau of Engraving and Printing—and you can go on a tour of the factory to see how it all happens. The federal government is the largest producer of currency in the world, and all paper bills are produced in just two places—Washington, DC, and Fort Worth, Texas. Take a forty-minute guided tour of the factory in the nation's capital, which shows the four-step process for making money. The factory looks very much like what you'd expect a factory to look like—with massive machines and real people on the floor running it all—but it's actually very modern, with incredible security measures deployed at every step. Visitors look down on the factory through glass windows and watch the money go from blank pages to finished bills ready to be shipped to Federal Reserve banks throughout the country. More than $500 million is produced here each day (but, no, they don't give out free samples!), and a tour of the factory is something you'll remember each time you open your wallet.

Bureau of Engraving and Printing
301 Fourteenth St. SW, 866-874-2330
moneyfactory.gov
Metro: Smithsonian (Orange, Silver, Blue Lines)

EXPLORE THE WORLD'S
LARGEST SHAKESPEARE COLLECTION

The Folger Shakespeare Library is home to the world's largest collection of the Bard's world-renowned works and attracts Shakespeare scholars from around the globe, but nonscholastic Shakespeare fans can also get a glimpse of his inspiring words with a guided tour. On Saturdays and Sundays, the Paster Reading Room is open for one hour to docent-led tours. The gorgeous, wood-paneled room houses many of his writings, along with a bust of Shakespeare and Nicola D'Ascenzo's famous stained glass window *Seven Ages of Man*. Tours are free, but advance reservations are required. Additional tours include a look at the architecture of the library itself and the outdoor Elizabethan gardens during warmer months. Visitors can also experience the library by taking in a Shakespeare or Shakespeare-inspired play in the award-winning Folger Theatre, and every year in April, the library celebrates the playwright's birthday with a family-friendly open house featuring sword-fighting demos, expert lectures, live music, and more.

Folger Shakespeare Library
201 East Capitol St. SE, 202-544-4600
folger.edu
Metro: Union Station (Red Line)

TOUR THE WORLD'S
LARGEST LIBRARY

How do you store 39 million books? That's how many the Library of Congress owns (and it's adding more every day!), along with 3.6 million recordings, nearly 15 million photographs, 5.5 million maps, 8.1 million pieces of sheet music, and 72 million manuscripts. All told, the Library of Congress holds more than 167 million items in its collection—which translates to a need for 838 miles of bookshelves. You won't see them all if you take a tour, but you will get a taste of how the nation's official library organizes and displays its vast collection. Visitors can take a one-hour docent-led tour of the Thomas Jefferson Building, where you'll learn about the art and architecture in the Great Hall and see researchers at work in the Main Reading Room. If you want to join the ranks of researchers, visitors over the age of sixteen can access the Main Reading Room by applying for a library card on-site.

Library of Congress
10 First St. SE, 202-707-5000
loc.gov
Metro: Capitol South (Orange, Silver, Blue Lines), Union Station (Red Line)

TIP
The Library of Congress celebrates reading with its annual National Book Festival (loc.gov/bookfest) at the Walter E. Washington Convention Center in late summer.

SEARCH FOR THE SCRIPTURES
IN THE CITY

Whatever your religious beliefs may be, the Museum of the Bible takes a compelling look at the enduring text. One of DC's newest museums, it aims to bring the Bible to life through in-depth exhibitions and interactive displays. Delve into the origins of the Old and New Testaments with walk-through experiences and theater presentations, explore the modern-day cultural influences of the Bible, and learn how the Gutenberg press democratized the distribution of the Bible. Bible buffs with a thrill-seeking side will appreciate the Washington Revelations attraction. The "flying theater" lets riders take a virtual tour of the engraved scriptures sprinkled throughout Washington, DC's famous monuments and memorials, from the Lincoln Memorial to the Library of Congress. End your visit with some reflection in the rooftop Biblical Garden and a delicious meal at Manna, which features gourmet offerings from critically acclaimed local chef Todd Grey.

Museum of the Bible
400 Fourth St. SW, 866-430-MOTB (6682)
museumofthebible.org
Metro: Federal Center SW (Orange, Silver, Blue Lines)

VISIT THE FINAL HOME
OF FREDERICK DOUGLASS

Once a slave in Maryland, abolitionist Frederick Douglass became one of the most influential African American leaders of the nineteenth century. He lived the last seventeen years of his life in the DC neighborhood of Anacostia at Cedar Hill. The home has been preserved as a National Historic Site and is open for guided tours. Led by National Park Service rangers, you'll view thirteen rooms, including the library where Douglass, a noted orator, wrote his speeches, books, and other works. A visitor center highlighting Douglass's life rounds out the tour. Cedar Hill sits atop a fifty-foot incline and offers one of the best views of DC in the city, so make sure to include some time to walk the grounds, soaking in both the history and the stunning view.

Frederick Douglass National Historic Site
1411 W St. SE, 202-246-5961
nps.gov/frdo
Metro: Anacostia (Green Line); transfer to the B2 bus to Mt. Rainier or the
V2 bus to Minnesota Ave.

TIP
The Smithsonian's Anacostia Community Museum is nearby.

CELEBRATE THE AMERICAN SPIRIT
AT ARENA STAGE

Perhaps Arena Stage's official vision statement says it best: its purpose is to "galvanize the transformative power of theater to understand who we are as Americans." The theater complex—it includes three different stages under one roof—produces plays that do just that. From classic American theater to cutting-edge new works by American playwrights, Arena Stage has been celebrating and exploring the American spirit since its inception in 1950. Although devoted to regional theater, Arena has become a launchpad for Broadway, with twenty-two shows and counting going on to the Great White Way, including *Dear Evan Hansen*, the 2017 Tony Award winner for best musical. Whether you see a show here that's bound for Broadway or one that creates a buzz only in DC, it's a must-visit venue for true theater buffs.

Arena Stage
1101 Sixth St. SW, 202-554-9066
arenastage.org
Metro: Waterfront-SEU (Green Line)

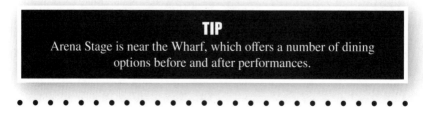

TIP
Arena Stage is near the Wharf, which offers a number of dining options before and after performances.

START YOUR SIGHTSEEING
AT THE SMITHSONIAN CASTLE

In 1826, a British scientist named James Smithson willed his entire estate to the United States with the caveat that the money must be used to create the Smithsonian Institution in Washington, DC, with the mission of the "diffusion of knowledge among men." His gift led to what is today the world's largest museum and research complex. First-time visitors to DC may not realize that the Smithsonian actually consists of nineteen museums (including two in New York City) and the National Zoo. For those who want to get their bearings before diving in, the Smithsonian Castle is the best place to start. Located centrally on the National Mall, it was the first Smithsonian building constructed (and where James Smithson's crypt is located). It serves as a visitor center, with an interactive touch-screen map of the Smithsonian complex along with several permanent exhibits that offer a glimpse into what's in store at the various Smithsonian museums. A café and small gift shop also make the Castle a convenient place for a sightseeing break.

The Smithsonian Castle
1000 Jefferson Dr. SW
si.edu/museums/smithsonian-institution-building
Metro: Smithsonian (Orange, Silver, Blue Lines)

REMEMBER MARTIN LUTHER KING JR.
AT HIS MEMORIAL

Standing tall along the Tidal Basin is a thirty-foot statue of Dr. Martin Luther King Jr. Arms crossed and gazing out over the water, the stone statue shares a sightline with both the Lincoln and Thomas Jefferson Memorials, placing the civil rights leader on equal footing with these other great American leaders. The statue appears to emerge from two boulders, known as the Mountain of Despair, a reference to Dr. King's most famous speech, "I Have a Dream." Engraved into one of the boulders is a quote from that speech, "Out of the mountain of despair, a stone of hope," serving as a reminder of Dr. King's uplifting leadership during the civil rights era. In addition to MLK's likeness, visitors to the memorial will also find a 450-foot-long inscription wall, which features fourteen inspiring quotes from Dr. King's history-making speeches, sermons, and other writings. The memorial is impressive both day and night but feels particularly reflective after dark with dramatic uplighting illuminating the statue of Dr. King.

Martin Luther King, Jr. Memorial
1964 Independence Ave. SW, 202-426-6841
nps.gov/mlkm
Metro: Smithsonian (Orange, Silver, Blue Lines)

GO AROUND THE GLOBE
WITH NATIONAL GEOGRAPHIC

National Geographic magazine has been giving would-be explorers a front-row seat to the world's most travel-worthy destinations for decades. The popular magazine is actually based in DC, and its headquarters include an on-site museum and event venue. Rotating, interactive exhibitions in the museum, along with lectures, movies, and other events as part of its Nat Geo Live series, bring the pages of the publication to life for visitors. There's always something going on that's sure to ignite the travel bug for fans of the magazine. The museum's permanent exhibition, *National Geographic: Exploration Starts Here*, is a great place to start your visit. It takes a look at the magazine's adventurous history through the eyes of its explorers, photographers, and reporters. You'll feel like you're along for the ride with video from the top of Mount Everest to Jane Goodall's research camp.

National Geographic Museum
1145 Seventeenth St. NW, 202-857-7700
nationalgeographic.org/dc
Metro: Farragut North (Red Line)

TAKE A BREAK FROM POLITICS
AT THE UNITED STATES BOTANIC GARDEN

Nestled at the base of the U.S. Capitol Building sits a gorgeous garden conservatory. If you were passing by without knowing the lay of the land, the large glass building might look out of place, but it was actually a dream of several Founding Fathers, including Washington, Jefferson, and Madison, to have a garden that would promote the importance of plants and agriculture to the new nation. The United States Botanic Garden, which is one of the oldest in North America dating back to 1820, still serves that purpose today. It houses a number of different environments, from a rain forest to a rose garden and even a live butterfly garden. It's a peaceful place for a rest whether you're a busy politico or simply need some downtime from sightseeing.

United States Botanic Garden
100 Maryland Ave. SW, 202-225-8333
usbg.gov
Metro: Capitol South (Orange, Silver, Blue Lines),
Federal Center SW (Orange, Silver, Blue Lines)

Photo courtesy CityCenterDC

SHOPPING AND FASHION

LIVE OUT YOUR LUXURY SHOPPING FANTASIES
AT CITYCENTERDC

If there were ever a place to live out your shopping fantasies, CityCenterDC is it. This open-air luxury shopping district in the heart of downtown was tailor-made for a movie montage-style makeover. Opened in 2015, it includes dozens of stylish shops from luxury brands such as Hermés, Gucci, Dior, and Burberry, plus a bevy of high-profile restaurants, including Momofuko and Daniel Boulud's DBGB. If you're worried about the price tags, don't fret. It's worth the trip simply to window-shop and check out the seasonal art installations along CityCenterDC's main thoroughfare, Palmer Alley. Previous fun and fantastical installations have included a canopy of thousands of beach balls to celebrate summer and pink lanterns suspended overhead during cherry blossom season. Also along Palmer Alley, don't miss the towering digital video screen that serves as the shopping center's gateway and plays trippy footage (think rotating planets and brightly colored rainstorms) on a constant loop.

CityCenterDC
Tenth and H Sts. NW, 202-289-9000
citycenterdc.com
Metro: Metro Center (Red, Orange, Silver, Blue Lines)

SEE WHERE WASHINGTON LUMINARIES
SHOP FOR SPARKLERS

You may be wondering why a more-than-eight-thousand-square-foot jewelry store that runs the length of two city blocks would call itself Tiny Jewel Box. The answer? The iconic DC bauble boutique didn't always reside in such a vast space. The store's humble beginnings date back more than eighty-five years when the Rosenheim family opened—you guessed it—a tiny store in the National Press Building. Through the years, the family's dedication to craftsmanship in their custom jewelry-making business, along with an eye for finding up-and-coming jewelers (the senior Rosenheim was one of the first to partner with David Yurman and Paul Morelli), has attracted a who's who of official Washington, foreign dignitaries, and Hollywood elite. FDR was one of the first famous faces to shop there, and the Obamas were known to gift jewelry from the store to their friends (including the Queen of England!). Browse an array of pieces from established and up-and-coming jewelers and watchmakers—all fit for a VIP.

Tiny Jewel Box
1155 Connecticut Ave. NW, 202-393-2747
tinyjewelbox.com
Metro: Dupont Circle (Red Line)

SHOP FOR DC-CENTRIC SOUVENIRS
AT THE CITY'S BEST MUSEUM GIFT SHOPS

The nation's capital is home to some of the world's very best museums—and the accompanying gift shops are world class as well. Whether you're looking for an only-in-DC souvenir or want to get in some holiday shopping, chances are there's a museum that aligns with your interests. Try the National Gallery of Art for a mix of everything, from prints to jewelry to home decor inspired by the museum's collection of masterworks. The Smithsonian's museums offer something for everyone—whether you're looking for the enduringly popular astronaut freeze-dried ice cream from the Air and Space Museum or modern art-influenced gifts from the Hirshhorn Museum and Sculpture Garden. Architecture buffs will love the gift shop at the National Building Museum, while the jewelry, books, and gardening accessories at Hillwood Museum's gift shop were tailor-made for the glamour-loving museumgoers in your life.

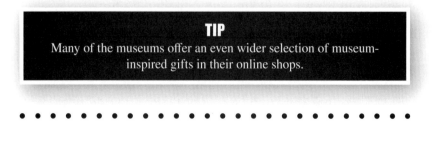

TIP
Many of the museums offer an even wider selection of museum-inspired gifts in their online shops.

MUSEUM-WORTHY SHOPPING

National Gallery of Art
Between Third and Ninth Sts. along Constitution Ave. NW
202-737-4215
nga.gov

Smithsonian National Air and Space Museum
Independence Ave. and Sixth St. SW, 202-633-2214
airandspace.si.edu

Smithsonian Hirshhorn Museum and Sculpture Garden
Independence Ave. and Seventh St. SW, 202-633-4674

National Building Museum
401 F St. NW, 202-272-2448
nbm.org

Hillwood Estate, Museum & Gardens
4155 Linnean Ave. NW, 202-686-5807
hillwoodmuseum.org

STROLL AND SHOP
ALONG GEORGETOWN'S M STREET

DC's oldest neighborhood is also one of its most prestigious. The preppy neighborhood that John F. Kennedy once called home is anchored by its namesake university and features a mix of small boutiques, luxury retailers, interior design studios, and art galleries—all set against a backdrop of Federal architecture and charming cobblestone side streets. Georgetown's main thoroughfare is M Street, a stretch of about eight blocks that runs from the Key Bridge to Rock Creek Parkway. Here you'll find all manner of well-known retailers, from Billy Reid and Brooks Brothers to Anthropologie and Kate Spade, plus plenty of restaurants when you need a retail break. Wisconsin Avenue bisects M Street (look for the historic gold-domed bank) and features even more shopping options. Don't miss Book Hill at the top of Wisconsin, a picturesque mix of rowhouses that includes art galleries, antique stores, and local shops. Every April the two-block area hosts the French Market, a three-day affair that transforms the sidewalks into an open-air market filled with finds from shop owners.

Georgetown
georgetownbid.com
Metro: Foggy Bottom-GWU (Orange, Silver, Blue Lines)

STEP BACK IN TIME
FOR ORIGINAL FINDS IN OLD TOWN
ALEXANDRIA

In a word, Old Town Alexandria—located just across the Potomac River in suburban Virginia—is quaint. The riverfront neighborhood with the small-town feel is home to a mixture of local boutiques and restaurants lining King Street. The neighborhood works hard to stay true to its colonial roots, meaning that retail and restaurant fronts are held to aesthetic standards that are similar to the eighteenth-century rowhouses. Add a few cobblestone streets for good measure and it's easy to see why "quaint" is a perfect descriptor. Old Town has also become a go-to for homegrown boutiques, making it a great destination to shop local. Start at the top of King Street near the Metro stop and meander your way down to the river, stopping to explore the shops on the main drag and the side streets along the way. Look for a mix of clothing boutiques, home decor shops, art galleries, and plenty of antique stores that are sure to turn up a treasure or two.

Old Town Alexandria
visitalexandriava.com
Metro: King Street-Old Town (Blue, Yellow Lines)

SNAP UP THE LATEST BEST-SELLER
AT POLITICS AND PROSE

In a company town like Washington, perhaps it shouldn't come as a surprise that a bookstore with the word "politics" right in the title continues to thrive even as e-commerce and big-box bookstores eat up the competition. Politics and Prose has been a mainstay on Connecticut Avenue for more than thirty years, stocking a diverse array of books on everything from yes, politics, to all manner of fiction and nonfiction, but it's the exhaustive calendar of author talks and events that keeps this bookstore buzzing. Nearly every night of the week and multiple events on the weekends draw DC's literati crowd, whether it's a reading of the latest blockbuster political tome to more intimate events with niche authors. Check the calendar before you go to see which author you'd like the chance to meet and greet.

Politics and Prose
5015 Connecticut Ave. NW, 202-364-1919
politics-prose.com
Metro: Van Ness-UDC (Red Line)

TURN THE PAGE

Browse the shelves at these local bookstores:

Kramerbooks
1517 Connecticut Ave. NW
202-387-1400
kramers.com

Idle Time Books
2467 Eighteenth St. NW
202-232-4774

Busboys and Poets
Multiple locations
busboysandpoets.com

TIP

Politics and Prose also has outposts at the Wharf
and Union Market. Both boast a full calendar
of literary events.

EXPLORE THE CITY'S OLDEST MARKETPLACE

Around since 1873, Eastern Market on Capitol Hill has been a gathering place for DC denizens for nearly 150 years. The South Hall is a cavernous brick building lined with food stalls offering everything from delicious apple pies to locally sourced meats to fresh flowers. Stock up on groceries or give the Market Lunch a try. Locals line up on weekends to devour its delicious—and locally famous—"blue bucks" (blueberry buckwheat pancakes). On the weekends, Eastern Market is particularly lively. Outside, row after row of vendors set up to ply their wares. Look for everything from original paintings of DC to handmade jewelry to pottery—all crafted by local artists. A farmers market with colorful fruits and vegetables also adds to the atmosphere outside on weekends, as do local musicians who help set the mood.

Eastern Market
225 Seventh St. SE, 202-698-5253
easternmarket-dc.org
Metro: Eastern Market (Orange, Blue Lines)

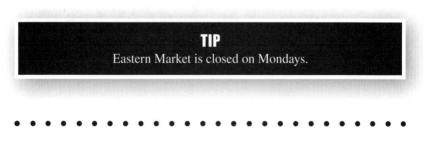

TIP
Eastern Market is closed on Mondays.

GET INSPIRED
BY BROOKLAND'S INDIE ARTISTS
ON THIRD THURSDAYS

DC may be known as the home of politicians, pundits, and the press, but the city also attracts a growing creative class of independent artists, designers, and other tastemakers. In Brookland (a Northeast neighborhood near Catholic University), get a glimpse of DC's artistic side at the Arts Walk, a pedestrian thoroughfare that features more than two dozen cozy art studios that double as shops, featuring works in the fine arts, photography, printmaking, sculpture, and more. Each studio keeps its own hours, but on Third Thursdays, most throw open their doors (or raise their garage doors, to be more accurate). Spend an evening browsing unique art, chatting with local artists, listening to live music, and dining at nearby cafés.

The Arts Walk
Monroe Street Market
716 Monroe St. NE, 202-640-4755
monroestreetmarket.com/arts
Metro: Brookland-CUA (Red Line)

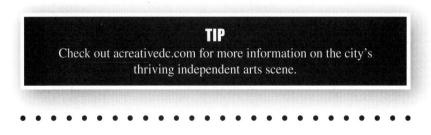

TIP
Check out acreativedc.com for more information on the city's thriving independent arts scene.

PURCHASE SOME POP ART
FROM LOCAL ARTIST MAGGIE O'NEILL

Much of the art depicting Washington, DC's famous monuments and memorials is fairly traditional, but there's one local artist who has put a distinctive spin on the city's iconic landmarks. Artist Maggie O'Neill has made a name for herself with her impressionistic pop art paintings of the Lincoln Memorial, the U.S. Capitol, and other DC-centric scenes. Her pop art political portraits have even scored her some high-profile fans, including none other than former President Obama, of whom she painted (and to whom she personally presented!) a portrait in 2012. You can see her work at her DC studio on weekdays and by appointment on weekends, or check out her latest original paintings and limited edition prints on her website. Her work is a must for anyone who loves politics—but doesn't take it too seriously!

Maggie O'Neill Studio
1525 Ninth St. NW
maggieo.com
Metro: Shaw-Howard U (Yellow, Green Lines)

SUGGESTED
ITINERARIES

FAMILY FUN

LUXURY

PATRIOTIC

GIRLS WEEKEND

ACTIVITIES
BY SEASON

SPRING

Be Enchanted by the Pink Petals at the National Cherry Blossom Festival, 31

Put Your Pinky Up at the Willard, 24

Explore the World's Largest Shakespeare Collection, 113

Have a Beer with Liz Taylor in Shaw, 12

Get a New View of the Memorials from the Water, 67

SUMMER

Pack a Picnic and Enjoy the Sounds of Summer at Wolf Trap, 30

Celebrate the Nation's Birthday with Fireworks on the National Mall, 36

Spend a Summer Evening Listening to Jazz in a Sculpture Garden, 34

Watch an Army Band Concert at Sunset, 44

Sway to the Sounds of Jazz in the Summer, 48

Dine al Fresco with 4,500 of Your Closest Friends, 22

Celebrate Summer at the National Building Museum, 46

Watch the Presidents Race at Nationals Park, 60

Watch Thousands of Motorcycles Converge on Constitution Avenue, 40

Roll Out Your Sleeping Bag at the Smithsonian, 92

Take a Spin around the Globe without Leaving DC, 110

FALL

WINTER

INDEX